CW01198208

FRANCIS FRITH'S

STAINES - A HISTORY AND CELEBRATION

THE FRANCIS FRITH COLLECTION

www.francisfrith.com

STAINES

A HISTORY AND CELEBRATION
OF THE TOWN

RUSSELL THOMPSON

THE FRANCIS FRITH COLLECTION

www.francisfrith.com

First published in the United Kingdom in 2004
by The Francis Frith Collection®

Hardback edition 2004 ISBN 1-90493-846-9
Paperback edition 2012 ISBN 978-1-84589-655-3

Text and Design copyright © The Francis Frith Collection®
Photographs copyright © The Francis Frith Collection®
except where indicated

The Frith® photographs and the Frith® logo are reproduced under licence from Heritage Photographic Resources Ltd, the owners of the Frith® archive and trademarks
'The Francis Frith Collection', 'Francis Frith' and 'Frith' are registered trademarks of Heritage Photographic Resources Ltd.

All rights reserved. No photograph in this publication may be sold to a third party other than in the original form of this publication, or framed for sale to a third party. No parts of this publication may be reproduced, stored in a retrieval system, or transmitted, in any form, or by any means, electronic, mechanical, photocopying, recording or otherwise, without the prior permission of the publishers and copyright holder.

British Library Cataloguing in Publication Data

Staines - A History and Celebration of the Town
Russell Thompson

The Francis Frith Collection®
Oakley Business Park, Wylye Road,
Dinton, Wiltshire SP3 5EU
Tel: +44 (0) 1722 716 376
Email: info@francisfrith.co.uk
www.francisfrith.com

Printed and bound in Great Britain
Contains material sourced from responsibly managed forests

Front Cover: **STAINES, BELL WEIR LOCK 1907** 58000t

Additional photographs by Russell Thompson.

Domesday extract used in timeline by kind permission of
Alecto Historical Editions, www.domesdaybook.org
Aerial photographs reproduced under licence from
Simmons Aerofilms Limited.
Historical Ordnance Survey maps reproduced under licence from
Homecheck.co.uk

Every attempt has been made to contact copyright holders of illustrative material. We will be happy to give full acknowledgement in future editions for any items not credited. Any information should be directed to The Francis Frith Collection.

The colour-tinting in this book is for illustrative purposes only,
and is not intended to be historically accurate

AS WITH ANY HISTORICAL DATABASE, THE FRANCIS FRITH ARCHIVE IS CONSTANTLY BEING CORRECTED AND IMPROVED, AND THE PUBLISHERS WOULD WELCOME INFORMATION ON OMISSIONS OR INACCURACIES

Contents

6	Timeline
8	Chapter 1 : At the Bridges
28	Chapter 2 : Growing Staines
48	Chapter 3 : Victorian Staines
78	Chapter 4 : 20th Century Staines
108	Chapter 5 : Looking Forward
121	Free Mounted Print Offer

STAINES FROM THE AIR 1928 AF23490

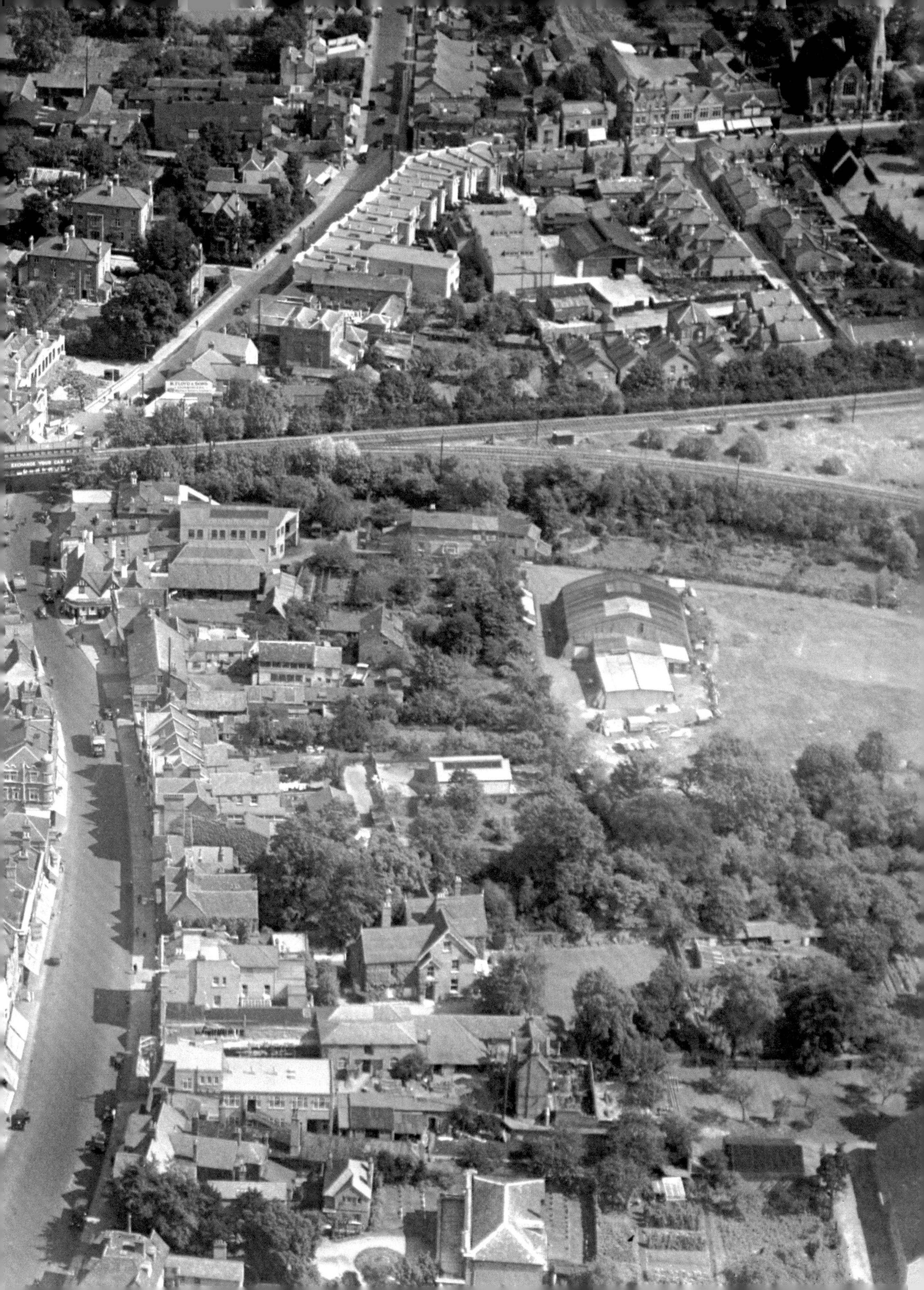

STAINES– *a history and celebration of the town*

Historical Timeline for Staines

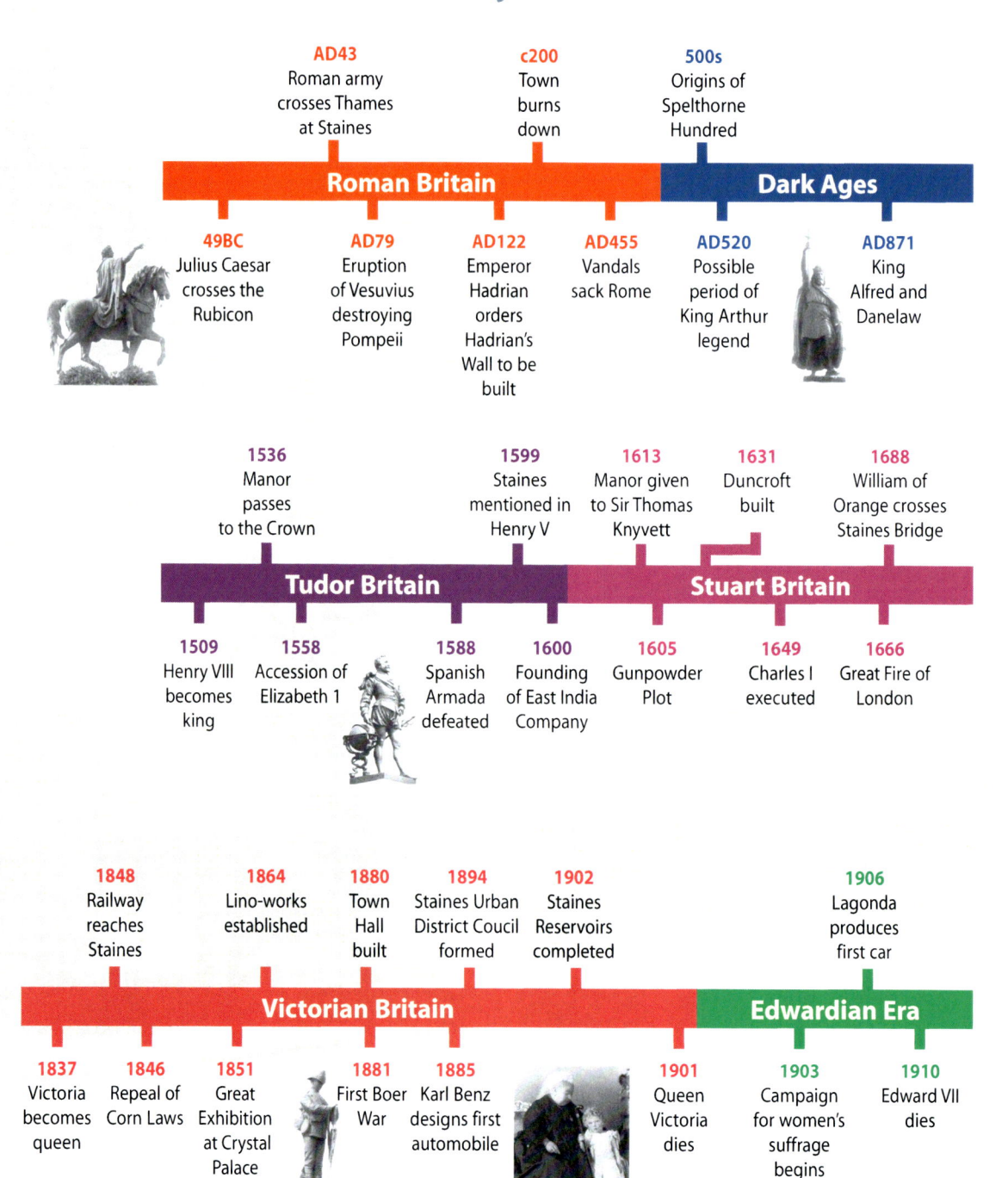

Roman Britain

- **AD43** Roman army crosses Thames at Staines
- **c200** Town burns down
- **49BC** Julius Caesar crosses the Rubicon
- **AD79** Eruption of Vesuvius destroying Pompeii
- **AD122** Emperor Hadrian orders Hadrian's Wall to be built
- **AD455** Vandals sack Rome

Dark Ages

- **500s** Origins of Spelthorne Hundred
- **AD520** Possible period of King Arthur legend
- **AD871** King Alfred and Danelaw

Tudor Britain

- **1536** Manor passes to the Crown
- **1599** Staines mentioned in Henry V
- **1509** Henry VIII becomes king
- **1558** Accession of Elizabeth 1
- **1588** Spanish Armada defeated
- **1600** Founding of East India Company

Stuart Britain

- **1613** Manor given to Sir Thomas Knyvett
- **1631** Duncroft built
- **1688** William of Orange crosses Staines Bridge
- **1605** Gunpowder Plot
- **1649** Charles I executed
- **1666** Great Fire of London

Victorian Britain

- **1848** Railway reaches Staines
- **1864** Lino-works established
- **1880** Town Hall built
- **1894** Staines Urban District Coucil formed
- **1902** Staines Reservoirs completed
- **1837** Victoria becomes queen
- **1846** Repeal of Corn Laws
- **1851** Great Exhibition at Crystal Palace
- **1881** First Boer War
- **1885** Karl Benz designs first automobile
- **1901** Queen Victoria dies

Edwardian Era

- **1906** Lagonda produces first car
- **1903** Campaign for women's suffrage begins
- **1910** Edward VII dies

Middle Ages

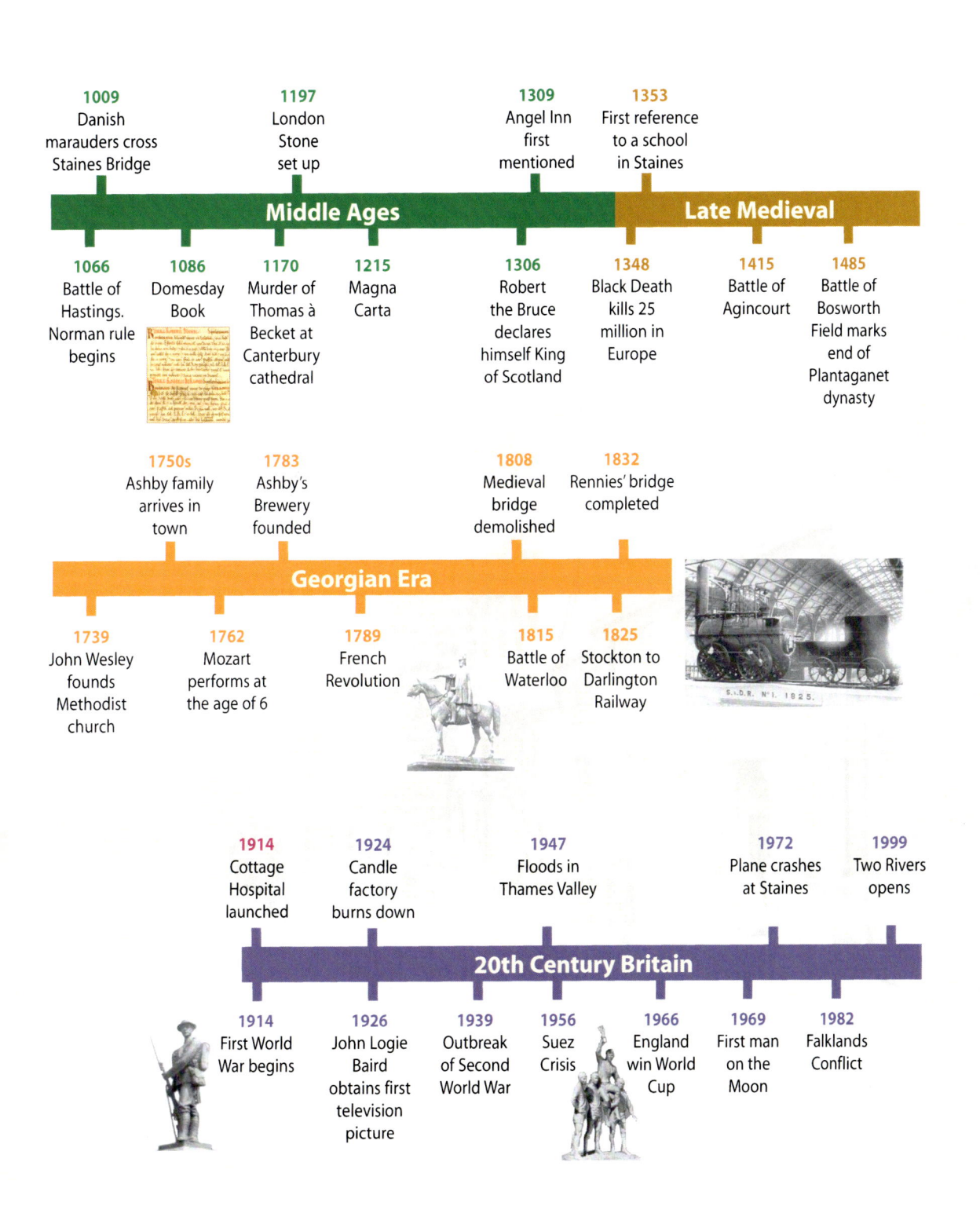

- **1009** Danish marauders cross Staines Bridge
- **1066** Battle of Hastings. Norman rule begins
- **1086** Domesday Book
- **1170** Murder of Thomas à Becket at Canterbury cathedral
- **1197** London Stone set up
- **1215** Magna Carta
- **1306** Robert the Bruce declares himself King of Scotland
- **1309** Angel Inn first mentioned

Late Medieval

- **1348** Black Death kills 25 million in Europe
- **1353** First reference to a school in Staines
- **1415** Battle of Agincourt
- **1485** Battle of Bosworth Field marks end of Plantaganet dynasty

Georgian Era

- **1739** John Wesley founds Methodist church
- **1750s** Ashby family arrives in town
- **1762** Mozart performs at the age of 6
- **1783** Ashby's Brewery founded
- **1789** French Revolution
- **1808** Medieval bridge demolished
- **1815** Battle of Waterloo
- **1825** Stockton to Darlington Railway
- **1832** Rennies' bridge completed

20th Century Britain

- **1914** Cottage Hospital launched
- **1914** First World War begins
- **1924** Candle factory burns down
- **1926** John Logie Baird obtains first television picture
- **1939** Outbreak of Second World War
- **1947** Floods in Thames Valley
- **1956** Suez Crisis
- **1966** England win World Cup
- **1969** First man on the Moon
- **1972** Plane crashes at Staines
- **1982** Falklands Conflict
- **1999** Two Rivers opens

CHAPTER ONE

At The Bridges

MENTION STAINES to the average UK resident, and the chances are that they will know it principally, if not solely, as the home of the television character Ali G. It is an association of which the town is half proud and half weary. The joke, of course, is an ironic one: that the fictional rapper, whilst harbouring aspirations to a certain kind of American street-cool, should actually hail from an unassuming little town on a picturesque stretch of the River Thames. A town whose economy was, until recently, heavily based on linoleum. A town that was once famed for its onion fair. It is not exactly the Bronx; nor, in all probability, would it wish to be.

At the beginning of the 21st century, Staines is typical of so many British towns: the pedestrianised High Street, the mix of Victorian civic grandeur and contemporary shopping-experiences, the catalogue of town-planning highs and lows, and yet its geography has, from the earliest times, given it something of a unique position. It is very much the gateway to and from London. Ali G may have put Staines on the map, but

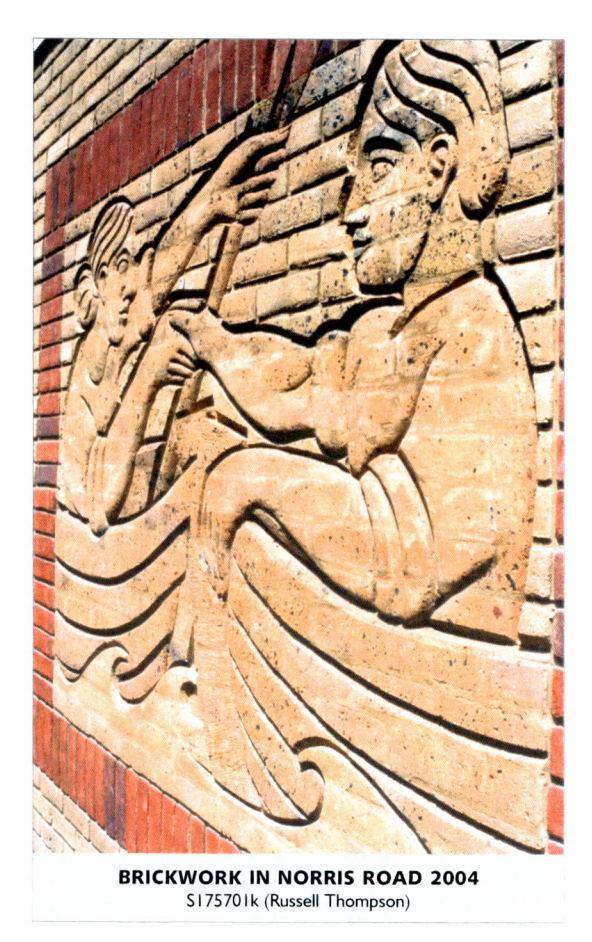

BRICKWORK IN NORRIS ROAD 2004
S175701k (Russell Thompson)

This brickwork relief in Norris Road represents the rivers Colne and Wraysbury, the two rivers of the eponymous shopping development.

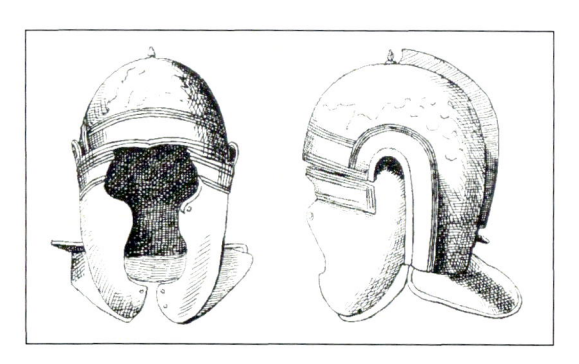

Artist's impression of a Roman helmet found in Germany
F6014

Staines was here before the map had even decided what shape it wanted to be.

Staines' story is intimately connected to the story of the Thames. The river itself started life as a drainage channel, carrying the meltwater at the end of the last great period of glaciation. In its current it transported alluvium and gravel, which it deposited at various points, throwing up banks and islands. It would then split into channels, meander around these obstacles it had made,

THE BRIDGE 1890 27256

Did you know?

Exciting Discovery

In the 1960s an exciting discovery was made at Yeoveney. It was what seemed to be an ancient burial-mound. People thought that it might be connected with the recently discovered Iron Age camp. The excitement ceased when somebody pointed out that the mound was, in fact, a target-butt belonging to the rifle-range that had closed in 1930. Human memory can be a very short-term thing.

and carry on to the sea. There was plenty of animal life here: the bones of a 50,000-year-old mastodon have been found on Staines Moor, and wherever there was game, there were probably hunters. There were certainly people living here, in the vicinity of what is now the High Street, by the third millennium BC. We have unearthed their flint tools and weapons - knives, awls, arrowheads - as well as fragments of their pottery. The Bronze Age, too, has left us with evidence of settlement in the form of urns and cooking vessels, both in Staines and also on the Egham side of the river. Traces were found of an Iron Age camp at Yeoveney, its position now submerged under one of the big reservoirs.

THE MOOR AT YEOVENEY 2004
S175702k (Russell Thompson)

Staines stands amidst a complicated network of rivers, at the point where the River Colne empties into the Thames. The Colne itself rises in Hertfordshire. It forks at West Drayton, and the other branch becomes the Wraysbury River, which rejoins the Colne near the bridge at Church Street in Staines. Another river, the Ash, is also linked to the lower reaches of the Colne. It meanders round the edge of Staines before flowing into the Thames. It has been repeatedly diverted by civil engineering projects; even its source had to be shifted when the Staines Bypass was built. Where it skirts Shepperton Studios, however, it has often proved useful for location work.

It is easy to see why people were attracted to the region, especially once they had grasped the concept of farming - because there were Iron Age farms, too, on Staines Moor. The various necks of the Thames had silted-up, leaving the gravel islands as one conjoined area that was ideal for cultivation. This is flat, fertile country, nicely irrigated without being waterlogged, and blessed with a humid climate.

The terrain would have been partly responsible, too, for the positioning of the long, straight road that was pushed westwards from London in the years immediately following the Roman conquest of AD 43. It had left the future capital at Newgate, running parallel to what is now Oxford Street, and passed through the areas of Shepherd's Bush and Hounslow before finally hitting the Thames. With marshy ground to the north and south, it was logical that the road would cross the

Staines' Rivers

Staines, From the Bridge 1890 23600

river in the middle of what we now call Staines. This was probably a crossing-point already. The Thames was much wider and shallower than it is today, and there may well have been a ford, ferry or rudimentary bridge here. Nevertheless, the Romans had soon constructed a bridge of their own: excavation has revealed the foundations of a stone bridgehead just behind the present Town Hall. The bridge may, initially at least, have been a wooden pontoon-like structure.

Caesar himself may have crossed the Thames here, though that honour is traditionally claimed by Lower Halliford.

Roman Staines was called Ad Pontes ('at the bridges'), or later, Pontibus (which means the same thing). It is not so much a name as a statement of fact, but the use of the plural is intriguing: perhaps there was still a midstream island, necessitating more than one bridge. Or perhaps the River Colne, too, had been bridged here.

14 STAINES – *a history and celebration of the town*

THE THAMES FROM THE BRIDGE c1960 S175021

The mouth of the Colne is just out of sight, beyond the tree. It was provided with a footbridge in the late 1980s, creating a continuous riverside path from Thames Street to the Lammas. Colne is a Celtic word that simply means 'river'.

Roman Staines, as seen in one of Gary Drostle's High Street mosaics

With the Roman invasion still new, and the Thames already marking the boundary between different British tribes, Ad Pontes was a politically sensitive place. The Romans would have placed some sort of checkpoint at the bridge. This soon expanded into a mansio, a military posting-station. Situated midway between London and the administrative centre at Calleva Atrebatum (Silchester), it was a convenient place for a night's stopover, and it soon developed into a small town. There were at least two streets of buildings: one on the line of the High Street, the other a little to the south. At the start of the second century, the predominantly wooden buildings began to be replaced by more permanent structures with stone foundations. Some had mosaic floors and painted plaster walls. As well as houses and provision-shops, there were workshops turning out leatherware, pottery and metal goods. The river, too, came into its own as a commercial thoroughfare: a series of wharves were constructed downstream from the bridge (where the Thames Street car-park is) dealing, maybe, with cargoes of stone, mineral ore, foodstuffs, ceramics, hunting-dogs and slaves. There was probably a market here, too; the area seems to have been good for raising pigs and cattle, and Ad Pontes would have been a suitable focal-point.

HIGH STREET MOSAIC 2004
S175703k (Russell Thompson)

The inhabitants, however, were not just workhorses. We know that they took pride in their appearance, because we have dug up items of their jewellery, including pins, brooches, and a splendid cameo-ring. We also know that they were a religious people: they seemed especially devoted to a goddess known as the 'dea nutrix', and left behind several effigies of her.

Towards the end of the second century, the town seems to have suffered some sort of disaster; a number of buildings in the High Street were burned down, others demolished. Perhaps the native tribes had revolted and torched the place, taking their lead from other insurrections that were then raging. A couple a decades later, there was a bad flood pushing the settlement further east towards what is now the Iron Bridge. It was not the last time Staines was to be beset by fire and floodwater. Ad Pontes rallied, though its focus was shifting; by the time that the legions were pulling out of Britain in the fifth century, the town had become more of an agglomeration of self-sufficient smallholdings.

ARTIST'S IMPRESSION OF RECONSTRUCTED SAXON HOUSES AT WEST STOW, SUFFOLK F6015

Did you know?
The Thames as a Deity

It is possible that the earliest settlers may have venerated the Thames as a deity. Beakers, swords and vases, perhaps hurled into the water as offerings, have been dragged from the river-bed at Staines and Egham. Most sources of water were worshipped in some way. This is where the Derbyshire custom of well-dressing comes from. Of course, we still personify London's river in the form of Old Father Thames.

A small village of Saxon incomers had sprung up outside the Roman town in the fourth century. The two settlements gradually became assimilated, culturally and probably racially. Saxon buildings were constructed on the sites of Roman buildings as, presumably, more Saxons colonised the area.

It was during this period, the Dark Ages, that this loose-knit farming settlement came to be known as Staines. The name means 'stones'. It has been suggested that these stones were the crumbled remains of the Roman town or, more specifically, of its bridge. The Saxons tended to view Roman ruins with a sense of baffled wonderment. On the other hand, there are one or two shadowy references to a nearby place called Negen Stana, generally interpreted as 'nine stones', and the name may be connected with this. If these stones existed (for there is no solid proof), they may have been tribal boundary-markers or they may, like other groups of stones, have had some sort of ritual purpose. They may have been stones of Roman significance that the Saxons were putting to some renewed use. The site is traditionally associated with that of St Mary's Church.

Stones or no stones, it was this outcrop of gravel, to the west of the Roman town, where Saxon Staines was concentrated. Saxons prefered areas of higher ground. This slight eminence around the church was known as Binbury, and in place-names, the element 'bury' denotes somewhere regarded as a fortress. That there was a church here prior to the Norman Conquest is probable; that it was founded in AD 675 by one Princess Erminildas of Mercia now seems unlikely, though the legend is perpetuated in a stained glass window in the present church. The error was based on the misreading of a manuscript that was actually referring to Stone in Staffordshire.

Saxon local government, such as it was, saw the country divided into shires. Staines fell within Middlesex, though the Thames was the boundary and Surrey sat just across the water. Shires were further subdivided into 'hundreds', each of which revolved around a meeting-point, a moot, where village elders would assemble on a regular basis and discuss matters of local concern.

This is the distant descendant of Staines' Saxon church. Four years after this photo was taken, the church lost its box-pews. The attractive Georgian galleries survived until 1947.

ST MARY'S CHURCH 1895 36004

At The Bridges   19

Saxon Spelthorne, by Gary Drostle.

The area bounded by Staines, Teddington and the Thames was, roughly speaking, the Spelthorne Hundred. The name, though not the precise boundary, is used by the modern borough. It seems to mean 'speech thorn-tree', meaning the site of the moot. It has been conjectured that this tree stood on Ashford Common, near the position of the present Spelthorne pub. This would make sense, as Ashford stood in the middle of the hundred.

The next time Staines crops up in the history-books it is, once again, as a crossing-point. Evidently there was still a bridge of some sort. The Anglo-Saxon Chronicle records that, in 1009, a horde of Danes had just pillaged Oxford and were now setting their sights on the capital. But 'when they had been warned that levies were waiting to oppose them at London, they crossed at Staines'. They seem to have left Staines unscathed. Just over fifty years later, however, England fell to the Danes' descendants, the Normans. Many places found themselves in the hands of new, Norman owners. Staines, though, belonged to the Abbot of Westminster, and would do until the Reformation. The Abbot appointed Staines' vicars. In return he required them to supply him with two large candles each year: these were placed on the altar at Westminster and burned on the eve of Epiphany.

HIGH STREET MOSAIC 2004
S175704k (Russell Thompson)

At The Bridges

The Wraysbury River sometimes awkwardly styles itself Wyrardisbury, taking its lead from the nearby village with the same choice of name. Here we see it in Hale Street, not far from where it used to drive Pound Mill.

There is a spurious tale that William the Conqueror, proceeding up the Thames, fancied Staines as the site of his new citadel, until one of his aides suggested Windsor

ARTIST'S IMPRESSION OF A NORMAN WARSHIP FROM THE BAYEUX TAPESTRY F6019

instead. Still, we know that the Conqueror sent his surveyors here, at least. He sent them everywhere, for the purpose of compiling his Domesday Book. Amongst other facts, this document tells us that Staines had no fewer than six watermills. Since the parish then included Ashford, Laleham, Halliford and Teddington, we can conclude that not all of these were in Staines proper. Strictly speaking, there were probably two mills here, Hale Mill and New Mill, which stood on the Colne and the Wraysbury respectively. Hale Mill survived for centuries; by the

THE WRAYSBURY RIVER 2004 S175705k (Russell Thompson)

1850s it was a papier-mâché factory. New Mill probably stood where Pound Mill was later built (immediately east of Staines West station). Both of these sites were eventually absorbed by Staines' huge linoleum-works.

At this point the manor of Staines also included the hamlet of Yeoveney, a mile up Moor Lane. The name, meaning 'Geofa's well-watered land', implied that the Saxon

> ## Did you know?
> ### Curious Structure
>
> *One of the most curious structures in Staines is the Cattle Bridge, just off Moor Lane. It is really three bridges stuck together, one after the other. The central portion, the oldest, spans the Wraysbury River. The two flanking sections were added later, to cross Staines' two railways. And just for good measure, the bridge also passes over the Staines Reservoirs Aqueduct, which runs alongside the disused West Drayton line.*

yeoman of that name had obviously been pleased with the way his crops were growing here, on the banks of the Wraysbury. At the most, the hamlet consisted of a manor house, its outbuildings, the Swan public-house and a small number of cottages. A small chapel once stood in the manorial farmyard. Most of the area that comprised Yeoveney has, since 1967, been inundated by Wraysbury Reservoir. Nonetheless, the manor's Gothick lodge-house still survives, and there is a cluster of houses at the point where Moor Lane (which once went all the way to Poyle) abruptly stops.

The first written reference to Staines parish church, St Mary's, occurs in 1179. The present structure has been greatly refashioned and bears little resemblance to what would then have been a simple nave-and-chancel building.

ST MARY'S CHURCH 1895 36002

Since its reconstruction in 1828, St Mary's Church has undergone few changes. It was rocked, however, by a bomb that fell in Wraysbury Road during the Second World War. As a result, the tower's pinnacles were felt to be no longer safe, and were taken down.

Magna Carta

John Lackland was what the book '1066 And All That' calls 'a Bad King'. Certainly he was a king who often abused his position. So, under the guidance of Stephen Langton, the Archbishop of Canterbury, John's barons drafted a charter that spelt-out the basic rights of the English citizenry. And at Runnymede (on the right in 23604), they forced the King to set his seal on it.

This great charter, the Magna Carta, recommended, amongst other clauses, that nobody should be punished without fair trial, and that justice was not a commodity that could be bought and sold. It also initiated the idea that a monarch could not increase taxation willy-nilly. However, it also reaffirmed the rights of the barons over their vassals, and is therefore often seen as a document that was simply protecting the status quo. It was by no means revolutionary.

EGHAM, RUNNYMEDE AND THE RIVER THAMES 1890 23604

EXAMPLE OF AN EXCERPT FROM THE MAGNA CARTA ZZZ00966

It certainly existed by 10 June 1215, though, when one of the key episodes in English history was being played-out on the other side of the Thames. There, just over a mile upstream, is Runnymede, the stretch of water-meadow where King John agreed to the demands of the Magna Carta. Although essentially a slight shifting of power between the monarchy and the aristocracy, Magna Carta showed that the Crown could be brought to book and, as such, it set a precedent for reforms to come.

Local tradition asserts that King John spent the previous night at Duncroft, a lavish house to the north of the church. As it was, the Duncroft estate had probably not been laid-out then and John would in any case have stayed at Windsor. Some of the other key-players may well have been lodging in Staines, though: it seems likely that the Archbishop of Canterbury took the opportunity to consecrate two bishops, those of Bangor and St David's, in Staines parish church.

The Norman and Angevin kings had their own vested interest in Staines. They had created a kind of private game-park in the Warren of Staines, the tract of wild scrubland between here and Brentford (Hounslow Heath, as it later became). Such places were called Royal Forests, which does not necessarily signify a heavy covering of trees. The Warren of Staines lost its status in 1227, although the area remained popular with royal hunting-parties.

John's successor, Henry III, granted Staines a fair in 1228: this was to be held annually on the four days following Ascension. Sixteen years later it was shifted to 7-10 September. A market had been founded here earlier the same century. Initially it was held on a Sunday, but in 1218, the Sheriff of Middlesex had ordered that this be changed to a Friday, an arrangement that held until the mid 19th century. Sunday trading was seemingly an issue even then. It is possible that the market was originally held in Church Street, at its widest point, but it soon became established at the western end of the High Street. One row of stalls became permanent fixtures: this was Middle Row, which (as the name suggests) sat in the road creating two carriageways until its demolition in 1802.

Henry III evidently had Staines' interests at heart, for he also granted the town a tree from Windsor Forest with which to repair its bridge. This was not the only time such concessions were made to Staines; on one occasion, forty years later, three oaks were granted in one go. We know, therefore, that Staines now had a wooden bridge. It stood somewhat downstream of the present bridge, connecting Market Square with the Swan at Egham Hythe (the pub in photograph 57991x). This medieval bridge seems to have been sturdily built, and Staines had cause to be grateful to it later, when subsequent bridge-building attempts proved relatively unsound. It is important to remember that, other than Kingston, this was the first bridge above London.

HIGH STREET MOSAIC 2004
S175724k (Russell Thompson)

At The Bridges

VIEW FROM THE BRIDGE 1907 57991x

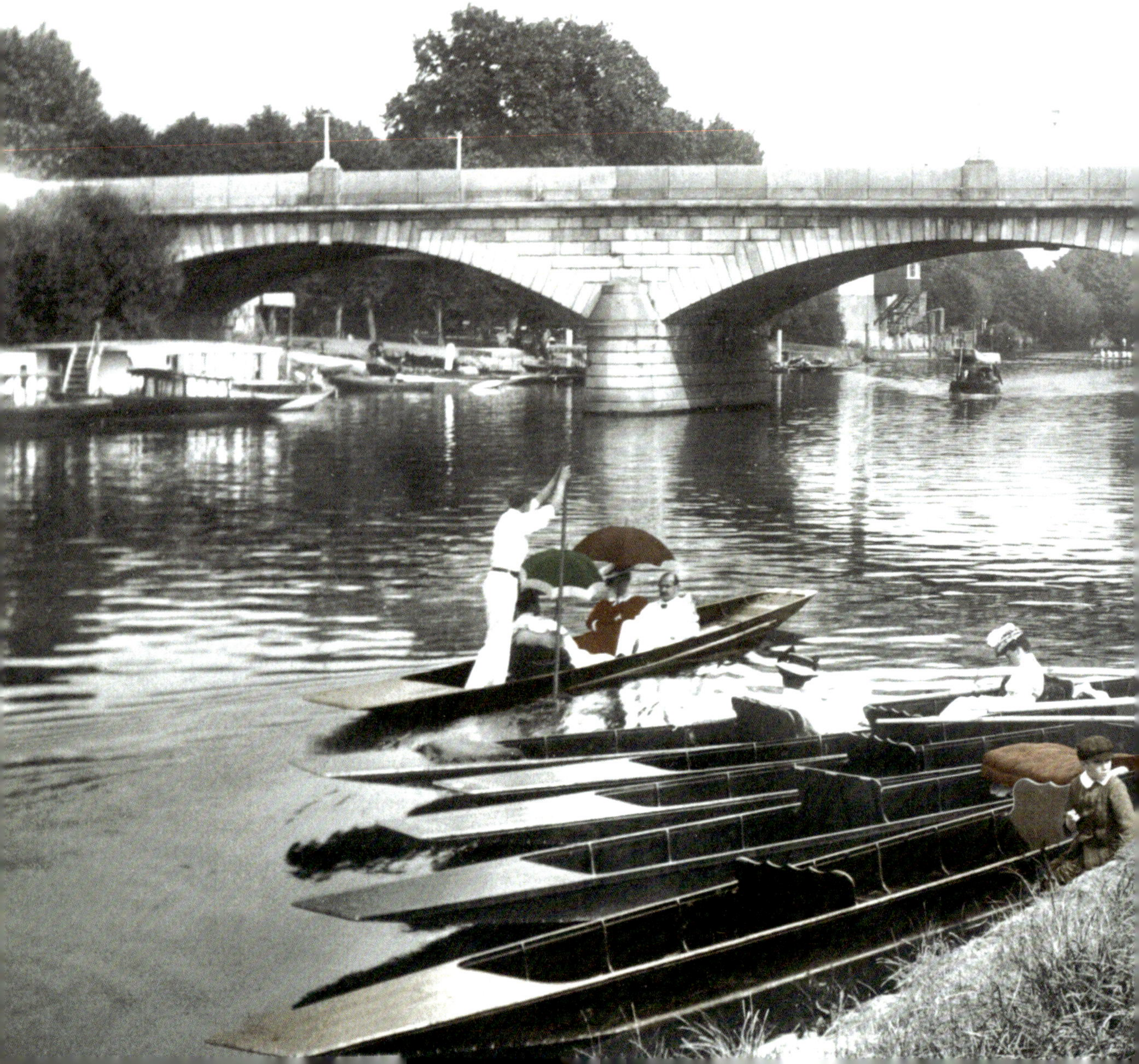

CHAPTER TWO

Growing Staines

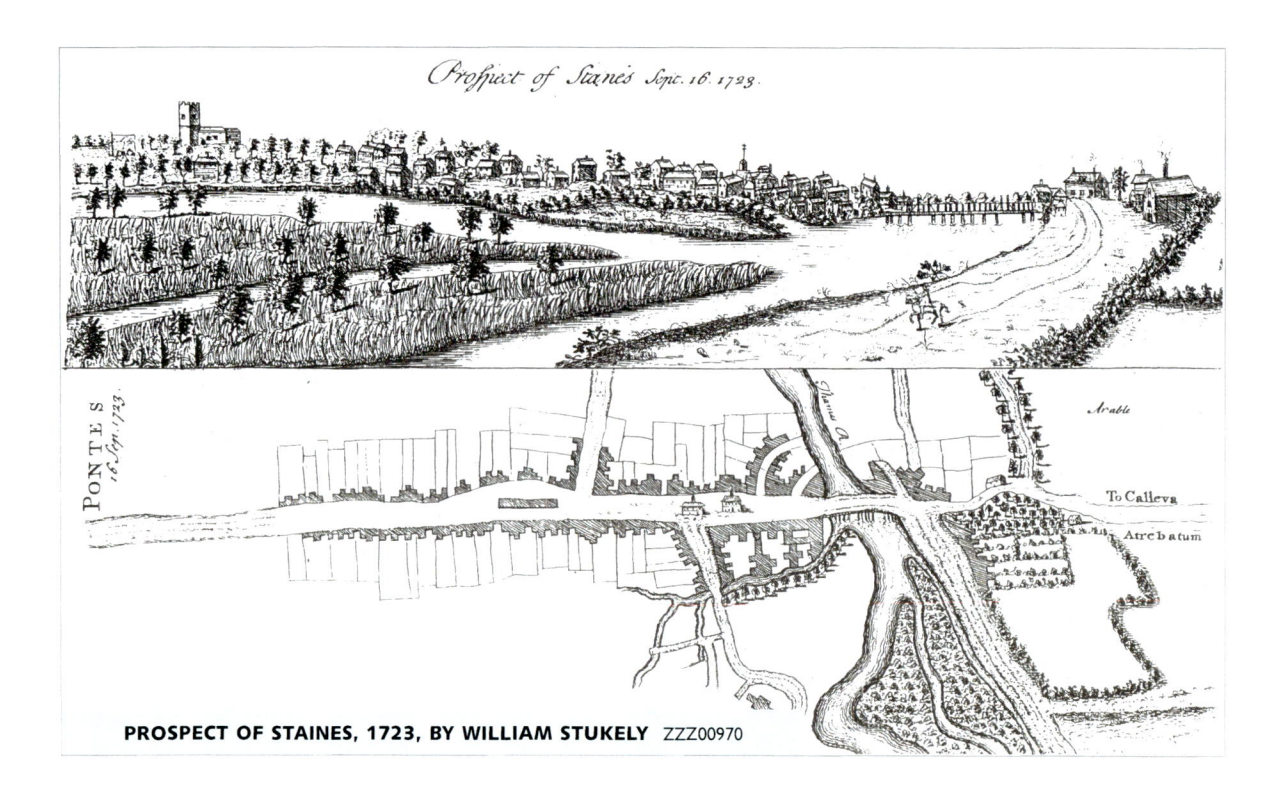

PROSPECT OF STAINES, 1723, BY WILLIAM STUKELY ZZZ00970

UNTIL THE 14th century, the Thames was tidal as far as Staines. The river was managed by the City of London, who had bought the prerogative from Richard I in 1197. They were not responsible for its entire length, though, and two small obelisks were set-up to mark the easternmost and westernmost limits of their jurisdiction. The former was the Crowstone at Prittlewell in Essex; the latter the London Stone at Staines. Shaped like a Roman altar, and later fitted with a plinth, the Stone has a rather iconic status in Staines. In its time, its image has graced school-badges, beer-labels, and the town's

Despite the fact that this is just a replica of the London Stone, it manages to look authentically ancient.

REPLICA OF THE LONDON STONE 2004
S175706k (Russell Thompson)

armorial bearings. It was apparently here by the 1280s, but it has been restored and re-inscribed on several occasions. There has probably been some version of it here since 1197. The London Stone we see today is a weather-beaten object, heavily abraded by, one assumes, generations of mooring-ropes. The lettering around its pediment once said 'God Preserve ye Citty of London', and we can still see the City's shield engraved upon it. These details suggest that the current Stone belongs to the tail-end of the medieval period.

It currently resides in the Town Hall, though a replica stands upstream at the Lammas, a tract of riverside land that was the Stone's home between the 1830s and 1986. Up until the 19th century, the London Stone and the Crowstone were both visited annually by the Lord Mayor.

The Lammas is interesting in itself. The name derives from 'Loaf Mass', a religious observation held each year on 1 August. This involved blessing a loaf of bread that had been made from the first grain harvested

THE LONDON STONE ZZZ00968

The Lammas lies just beyond Church Island. Colonised by bungalows in recent years, the island is linked to the shore by a footbridge, and by a manually-winched steel platform that is used for conveying heavy goods across the water.

VIEW FROM THE BRIDGE c1960 S175042

in the parish each year. The fields that traditionally provided these harvests were known as Lammas lands. At Staines, the Lammas, as a whole, extends either side of the Wraysbury Road, from Church Island to the Moor, and was for several centuries a fiercely guarded piece of common land.

It is at this point that the Thames still betrays vestiges of its old meandering ways. A glance at an Ordnance Survey map will reveal certain anomalies in the county, and constituency, boundaries around Staines. This is because, on both sides of the river, the boundaries follow watercourses that are now much less significant than they once were, or that have now vanished entirely. They are collectively known as the County Ditch. One part is the stream that forms the western edge of the Lammas, and still separates the modern counties of Surrey and Berkshire. The other section is the area of trading-estates on the opposite bank of the Thames from Church Island, which was historically included in the parish of Staines. It was once an island, and was where the osiers were grown that were integral to the town's basketmaking industry.

The Packhorse

PACKHORSE HOTEL 1895 35989

At one time, a large part of England's economy was based on the wool-trade. The road through Staines was a conduit for the packhorses bringing the wool from the West Country. When it arrived here, it was usually taken down the Thames and shipped to Holland. Unfortunately, the horses' progress into Staines was hindered by the marshy road skirting the south bank of the Thames. A 13th-century businessman, Thomas de Oxenford, took the matter in hand and rebuilt the road as a raised causeway. It is still called The Causeway today.

Near where the horses transferred their cargoes onto the boats, there was a pub called the Woolpack. It was later renamed the Packhorse. These wool-trade references imply that the pub predated its first appearance in written documents (1629). It is now called the Thames Lodge Hotel, and is thus rather shorn of its ancient connotations.

FAKE WINDOW AT THE BLUE ANCHOR PUB 2004
S175707k (Russell Thompson)

The Blue Anchor pub has five painted trompe-l'œil windows lurking amongst the real windows on its front. They replace five windows that were bricked-up in 1696 to avoid payment of the Window Tax, a bizarre imposition that was not repealed until 1851.

Westminster Abbey lost its ownership of Staines in 1536, at the dissolution of the monasteries, and for a while the manor belonged to the Crown. Henry VIII, its first royal owner, had designs on Staines; he planned to resurrect the royal hunting-ground that had once lain to the east of the town. We also know that he occasionally savoured some of the local delicacies. There is a record of him paying some Staines fishermen for a haul of salmon (from the Thames!). It is worth remembering that, even up until the 20th century, with its vogue for noisy boats, fishing was an important industry here.

Like all good thoroughfare towns, Staines was accumulating an impressive tally of inns. Documents of the 15th century mention the Cock, the Blue Anchor, the Bush, and the Angel. The Cock was in Church Street, and the Bush not far away at the approach to the bridge. Its name supposedly came from a tradition of hanging a bough of greenery outside an inn to indicate when the freshly-brewed beer was ready. The Blue Anchor, in Market Square, is ostensibly 18th-century, though a recent restoration uncovered a medieval oak beam. But it is the Angel that seems to have the earliest origins. There was an inn on this site in 1309, though it was not the present building. The name suggests ecclesiastical ownership - in this case, as with much of Staines, the Abbot and Convent of St Peter's, Westminster.

Did you know?

Shakespeare and Staines

In 1599, Shakespeare fleetingly dropped Staines' name into Henry V. At one point, Pistol's wife urges him to accompany her to Staines instead of following his band of brothers into the French warzone. Being Pistol, however, he is having none of it, and off he goes, though when we last see him he is on the battlefield being force-fed leeks by a frenzied Welshman. So perhaps he should have listened to his wife.

In 1613, James I unloaded Staines and one Thomas Knyvett became Lord of the Manor. He came from a family that had held various court positions since the 13th century, and Sir Thomas himself had served both under James and Elizabeth I. He already owned the manor of Stanwell. He was a Justice of the Peace and had been the man who, on 5 November 1605, had arrested Guy Fawkes and extracted the unhappy man's confession. It is not Knyvett, though, who has passed into folklore. He and his wife, a royal governess, are commemorated on a sculpted tomb in Stanwell church, resplendent in their Jacobean fashions. Stanwell had remained the Knyvetts' home and, although Staines had a manor house, very few Lords of the Manor ever lived there. Until its demolition in the 1970s it stood beside the River Ash, where Chestnut Manor Close was later built.

A local contemporary of Knyvett was one William Gillett. Dying in 1625, he left an annual allowance to cover the tuition fees of four poor children. There had been references to a school in Staines as early as 1353, although we do not know where it was or what form it took. At one point, Gillett's bequest was being paid to the parish clerk, who took care of the teaching. In 1808, it was redirected into the funds of the newly opened British School, and later went towards the choirboys of St Mary's Church.

The religious to-ing and fro-ing of the Tudor monarchs did not just affect the ownership of the manor. In 1549, there was an uprising in the West Country, prompted by the publication of Edward VI's new Prayer Book. At one point it was rumoured that Staines Bridge would be pulled down to head-off the mob, and the townspeople had to petition the Privy Council to not take such measures. Fortunately for most people concerned, the revolt was put down. In historical terms it was only a brief respite as the bridge was in fact cut during the Civil War. Once again, Staines was being viewed as an important strategic point, and the town was successively occupied by each of the opposing factions. There were scuffles on Staines Moor. The bridge was then replaced by a ferry.

One of the first things any eastbound invader would have seen in Staines, had he or she paused to admire the architecture, was the market-house. This was certainly in existence by the 1660s. Pictures show it as a small, two-storey, brick building. It had a wooden bell-turret for the market-bell, which would have been rung to announce the start of trading on market-days. The building had an open ground-floor, supported on columns: this was an area where transactions could be carried out. Sir Walter Raleigh is popularly supposed to have been tried here in 1603, for his alleged involvement in a plot to depose James I. In fact, the trial took place at Winchester. At the most, he probably just passed through Staines and was perhaps kept overnight at the market-house under lock and key.

Had Raleigh been left to his own devices, he may have opted to check-in at the Bush, just across the road. It was here that the town's better-off visitors often chose to stop.

Duncroft

DUNCROFT 1895 36011

Although the Duncroft estate dates from 1286, the present house belongs to the early 17th century. The grounds extended almost as far as Church Street, but were truncated by the building of Wraysbury Road in the 1950s.

Duncroft has a rather silly ghost story, which holds that a young black servant-boy was once drowned in a vat of boiling oil in the kitchen. His spirit then engaged in poltergeist activities around the house until an exorcism was held. There, the ghost stated that he would only rest if a road in Staines was named after him. Hence Blackboy Lane. The fact of the matter is that the lane was named after a long-vanished Black Boy pub. This was one of Charles II's nicknames ('black' then meant black-haired), and his Restoration in 1660 saw a spate of inns being named in his honour.

(Two hundred years later, Nelson stayed there, 'recuperating' with Lady Hamilton after the Battle of Copenhagen.) Being on such a major road, it was inevitable that Staines' inns would be used for accommodation, as well as for a variety of other functions. The Bush and the Angel acted as posting-houses, back in the days when handling the post was a duty that generally fell upon innkeepers. Both pubs also catered for the golden age of coaching. The Angel still has the archway that led to its stables. The Bush had even more extensive outbuildings: its premises stretched as far as Bridge Street and included much of the land that now lies between Clarence Street and the river.

Because the Bush was the closest inn to the bridge, it also played a strategic role. The Middlesex Militia had a permanent billet here. They had gathered at Staines in 1644, to defend London after the Second Battle of Newbury. Their presence was not warmly welcomed by the locals. The Angel, too, sometimes accommodated troops: a certain Captain Coward was stationed here in 1688, to oppose the invading William of Orange. The bridge had been patched-up again after the Restoration and properly rebuilt in the 1680s, but it was now once again threatened with a tactical demolition. This time, it was not carried out. In view of the ease with which William staged his Bloodless Revolution, it is conceivable that Captain Coward may just have lived up to his name. Whatever the truth of the matter, he never paid his stabling-fees at the Angel.

In many ways, Staines was the first landfall for westbound travellers after leaving London, and one that they were often relieved to make before dusk, as Hounslow Heath was notoriously infested with highwaymen. Where the road traversed the Heath, it was so ill-defined that a traveller could easily get disorientated. This once happened to Samuel Pepys, who had hired a guide to conduct him safely to Staines. The guide was seemingly in the wrong job, for he 'lost his way in the forest' and the journey took ages.

Coal-duties were originally introduced to help the City of London meet the costs of the Great Fire of 1666. They were not wiped out, however, until 1890. Anyone bringing coal into the City, past one of these boundary-posts, was required to pay a fee.

BOUNDARY POST 2004 S175708k (Russell Thompson)

CONGREGATIONAL CHAPEL 1895 36006

The Congregationalists, or the Independent Sect as they were initially called, had had a chapel in Tilly's Lane since 1789. They migrated to a new building in Thames Street in 1802. Thirty-five years later they demolished it and replaced it with the church in this photograph.

Roads were an ongoing problem. Henry VII once passed through Staines on a journey from Canterbury to Windsor, and was so appalled by the state of the roads that he gave £2,000 towards the repair of the entire route. Amongst other things, a poor road caused delays to the post. Soon after Pepys' visit, the Hounslow-Basingstoke section of the A30 (as it later became) was put in the hands of a turnpike trust.

It has been said that, for the most part, the lives of ordinary people were unaffected by the political upheavals of the 17th century, and it now seems evident that the people of Staines were more concerned about their trade-routes and communications than they were about the political and religious bias of the country. And it was around this time that Quakerism first appeared in the town. It seemed to cater for tradespeople; and these people, the middle classes by any other name, were increasingly becoming a force to be reckoned with. In Staines the Quakers were meeting in each other's houses by the 1660s, though it was not until 1715 that they acquired a purpose-built meeting-house. It was in Blackboy Lane, roughly where the Memorial Gardens now lie. Baptists, Congregationalists and Methodists established themselves a little later: all had some sort of meeting-house here by the last quarter of the 18th century (see 36006). John Wesley himself preached in a house in Kingston Road in 1771.

HIGH STREET 1895 35984

The lofty classical building on the right is Ashby's Bank. The family also owned the small structure next door; this was their wines and spirits emporium. Three houses along, above the bowed window, is the famous Golden Boy.

We must return to the Quakers, the Society of Friends, to give them their proper name, in order to meet Staines' most enterprising family. At their peak they seem to have accounted for a high percentage of the town's Quaker population. The Ashbys arrived in Staines in the 1750s in the form of Thomas, a mealman of limited means. The family were later to include mill-owners, bankers and wharfingers, but it is with brewing that we primarily associate them. Thomas Ashby's son, another Thomas, began brewing in his house, 57 Church Street, in 1783. He built a malthouse in his back garden, and was soon prospering. Nobody then saw anything paradoxical in a Quaker family being involved in the manufacture of alcohol. It was a respectable trade, and one that was not new to Staines. We have documentary evidence of a brewhouse in the town as early as 1301.

This second Thomas Ashby opened a bank in another Church Street house, just opposite his brewery, in 1794. Banking was still relatively open to all, and for a while Ashby's Bank issued its own notes (see 35984 above, by which time the bank had moved to the High Street). Today, Church Street retains many of its 18th- and 19th-century houses and would not, therefore, be wholly alien to the early members of this entrepreneurial family.

Down the road, at Staines Bridge, something else was brewing: trouble. In 1791, Parliament

THE MEDIEVAL BRIDGE IN 1795 ZZZ00972

Did you know?

Wellington's Brother

At the end of the 18th century, Staines' vicar was the Rev Gerald Wellesley. He was Wellington's younger brother and the Iron Duke occasionally attended church here during his incumbency. Perhaps he rubbed shoulders with Lady Letitia Lade, one of the Prince Regent's former mistresses. She lived at the Hythe and is buried at St Mary's. Her name was also romantically linked to that of 'Sixteen String' Jack Rann, a tiresomely foppish highwayman.

had passed an Act authorising the replacement of the much-abused medieval bridge. Traffic was on the increase and, in any case, architectural tastes were changing. The matter was put into the hands of one Thomas Sandby, a draughtsman with royal connections. His three-span bridge opened in 1797. Sandby, however, did not enjoy a high reputation. He was already dubbed 'Tommy Sandbanks' after one of his previous works, the dam at Virginia Water Lake, had disintegrated during a storm. The new bridge looked hardy enough (and was aesthetically satisfying enough for J M W Turner to sketch and paint it) but, within weeks, it began to sink. Fortunately the medieval bridge was still standing, and it was reopened whilst the Bridge Commissioners mused over their predicament.

Growing Staines

The Commissioners, a quango of fourteen men on whose shoulders the responsibility rested, resorted to 'plan B'. This involved an iron bridge made by one Thomas Wilson. Iron bridges were the latest craze, ever since the world's first one had arched its back at Coalbrookdale in Shropshire. The main span of Wilson's bridge already existed, in fact: it had been on display in Hyde Park as an example of the new technology. One interesting footnote is that it had supposedly been designed, in the first instance, by the social reformer Thomas Paine. It would seem that he was a man of many parts. Anyway, Wilson now cut this iron showpiece in half, and installed one segment at Staines, grafting it onto the approaches that Sandby's bridge had conveniently left behind (see 35988, page 42-43). It opened in 1803.

The Bridge Commissioners must have collectively held their heads in their hands when this bridge, too, developed problems. Cracks appeared (being cut in half had probably not helped) and once again the faithful old wooden bridge was called into service. Staines Bridge carried a universally unpopular toll for both road and river traffic and this was increased to finance the project's spiralling costs. The famous engineer John Rennie was asked to assess the situation. He had a number of bridges to his name (including Southwark and London), none of which had fallen down. Sadly, his quotes for a new Staines Bridge were deemed too expensive, so he and his two sons devised a way of shoring-up the broken iron bridge on forty-eight wooden piles. This in itself

THE IRON BRIDGE 1914 ZZZ00973

was not cheap. Nevertheless, the job was done and the bridge re-opened in December 1807. Contemporary illustrations show it as a bizarre-looking structure that was neither one thing nor another. Its struts constituted an obstacle to passing boats. The time was considered right, however, to finally dismantle the medieval bridge. Repair-costs for the shored-up iron bridge continued to rocket. Its death-knell came in 1827 when a cart belonging to George IV, pulled by no fewer than sixteen horses, attempted a kind of three-point turn whilst making the crossing. The hefty monarch was not personally on board, but the weight was sufficient to snap two of the bridge's major joists.

The Rennies were called in again. John Rennie was now dead, but his sons made plans for a new bridge. In so doing, they made a major break with tradition, by visualising it upstream of the traditional site. The previous bridges, it was decided, had perhaps been weakened by being downstream of the Thames' confluence with the River Colne; this had obviously greatly added to the volume of water battering against their piers.

Growing Staines 43

Before 1832, all of Staines' bridges crossed the river here. All that remains are traces of the stone abutments of Thomas Sandby's 1797 effort. They are embedded in the garden wall at the far left of this picture.

SWAN HOTEL AND BOAT-HOUSE 1895 35988p

THE BRIDGE 1895 35990

The work was begun in the spring of 1829, marked by a small ceremony on the Middlesex bank. On the Surrey side, at Egham Hythe, the foundation-stone was laid by the Duke of Clarence. On 23 April 1832 he returned, now as King William IV, and performed the opening ceremony. The new bridge was an elegant piece of engineering. It had three arches and was made of white Aberdeen granite (see 57990 and 35990). Just in case anybody got any ideas, a notice was affixed to the parapet: 'Any person wilfully injuring any part of this County Bridge will be guilty of Felony and upon Conviction be liable to be kept in Penal Servitude for Life'. This was fighting talk.

Growing Staines 45

THE BRIDGE 1907 57990p

PUNTING PEOPLE

PRETTY LADIES

Egham Hythe

Ye Olde Bridge House 1895 35987

'Hythe' is an old term for an inland port, somewhere on a river rather than on an estuary. It is the last syllable in several place-names, such as Lambeth and Rotherhithe. Effectively Staines' landing-place (though on the Surrey side of the river), Egham Hythe was already established at the end of the seventh century. The slight curvature of the Thames here provided it with some degree of shelter.

The Hythe's pubs, the Swan and the Ann Boleyn (the latter previously known as Ye Olde Bridge House), were once frequented by bargees. They could sometimes be rough places. The main street (photograph 35987) has been bypassed in recent years by the Petters roundabout. The Hythe was made a Conservation Area in 1969.

Growing Staines

COUNTY MAP OF MIDDLESEX c1850

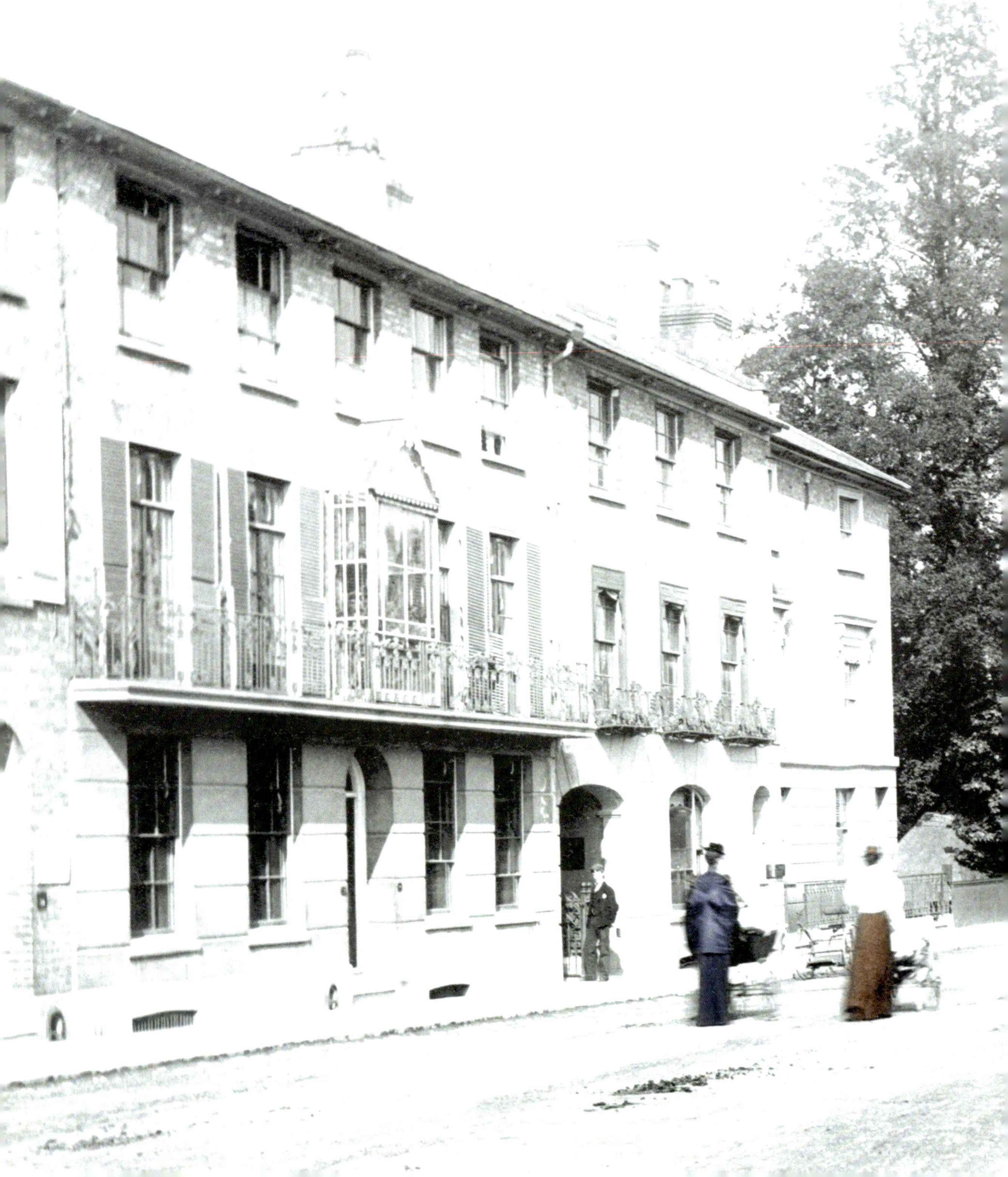

CHAPTER THREE

Victorian Staines

CLARENCE STREET 1895 35985p

VICTORIA was still five years away from the throne when the new bridge opened, but Staines was already being kickstarted into a new era. For a start, the old, familiar street-plan had been altered. There was a new road connecting the High Street with the Rennie bridge; broad, straight and voguish, this was named Clarence Street after the Duke (see 35985 and 35983). Another new road, Bridge Street, was pushed through to link the new crossing-point with Church Street. About twenty buildings, among them the Bush Inn, had to be pulled down to clear the approaches. Even the London Stone was moved out of the way, and relocated to the Lammas.

The authorities obviously saw it as a chance for an all-round purge. They widened the top of Thames Street in order to 'add to the comfort of those gentlemen who have frequently to pass up the said road' and who were 'otherwise obliged to wait for a considerable time before they can pass in safety'.

Staines, by the sound of it, was being gentrified. On this occasion, the town's fire-engine house, which stuck awkwardly into the roadway, was removed. But it was not the last time that the narrow entrance of Thames Street (or the Shooting-Off Road, as it was still called) would prove to be a nuisance.

HEADQUARTERS OF THE SHOWMEN'S GUILD 2004 S175709k (Russell Thompson)

This is now the headquarters of the Showmen's Guild, though it was built in 1835 as a Literary & Scientific Institute. It was subsequently a newspaper office, a piano showroom, and a Liberal Club, though not all at the same time. Between 1950 and 1979, it housed the public library.

The Bush, as it happened, rose again. The name, with a little adjustment, was transferred to a new hostelry in Clarence Street, the Bush & Clarence. Like its forebear, it was a fairly extensive building, and had a second entrance in Church Street. In fact, it was this rear half that survived as a pub when the Clarence Street section was converted into a private residence. The pub still flourishes, though it was renamed the Hobgoblin in 1992, an unpopular move with history-conscious locals.

Perhaps sensing the way the wind was blowing, literally and metaphorically, a large chunk of St Mary's Church had collapsed during evensong on a wet Sunday in 1826. Nobody was hurt, a fact that rested on the poor weather having kept the bulk of the congregation at home. It was decided to rebuild the entire church, except for the fine red-brick tower of 1631 (which, according to an attached inscription, was built by Inigo Jones, though this attribution is generally regarded as spurious, since the plaque only appeared in 1791). The building was now getting too small for the town's burgeoning population. When the revised church was opened in 1829, it had sufficient space for 1,000 worshippers.

The corner-building on the right was later occupied by George Perkins, an eccentric butcher who installed a goldfish-pond beside his counter. Midway up Clarence Street, by the trees, the road crosses the River Colne. This diminutive bridge was also built by the Rennies.

CLARENCE STREET 1895 35983p

By the 1830s there were other rumblings afoot that would seriously undermine Staines' shiny new image. Roads and rivers were no longer the only arteries of traffic, and much of Staines' passing trade was being removed by the railways. The City of London had annulled all river-tolls in 1834, but there was still a toll for anything crossing the bridge. As well as fees for carts and coaches, there was a 6d charge for each chaise, or individual horse or cow that went across. However, the revenue was dwindling. It all seemed to happen very fast, and Staines had become something of a ghost town by the 1840s. It was calculated that fewer than a dozen coaches now passed through each day, as opposed to the seventy-odd of recent years. Much of the remaining traffic was local, and it was therefore the townspeople who paid most of the toll-money. Some years earlier, the Bridge Commissioners had sensibly leased the toll-collection to a third party and washed their hands of the matter.

54   STAINES – *a history and celebration of the town*

ST MARY'S CHURCH, FROM THE RIVER 1895 36005

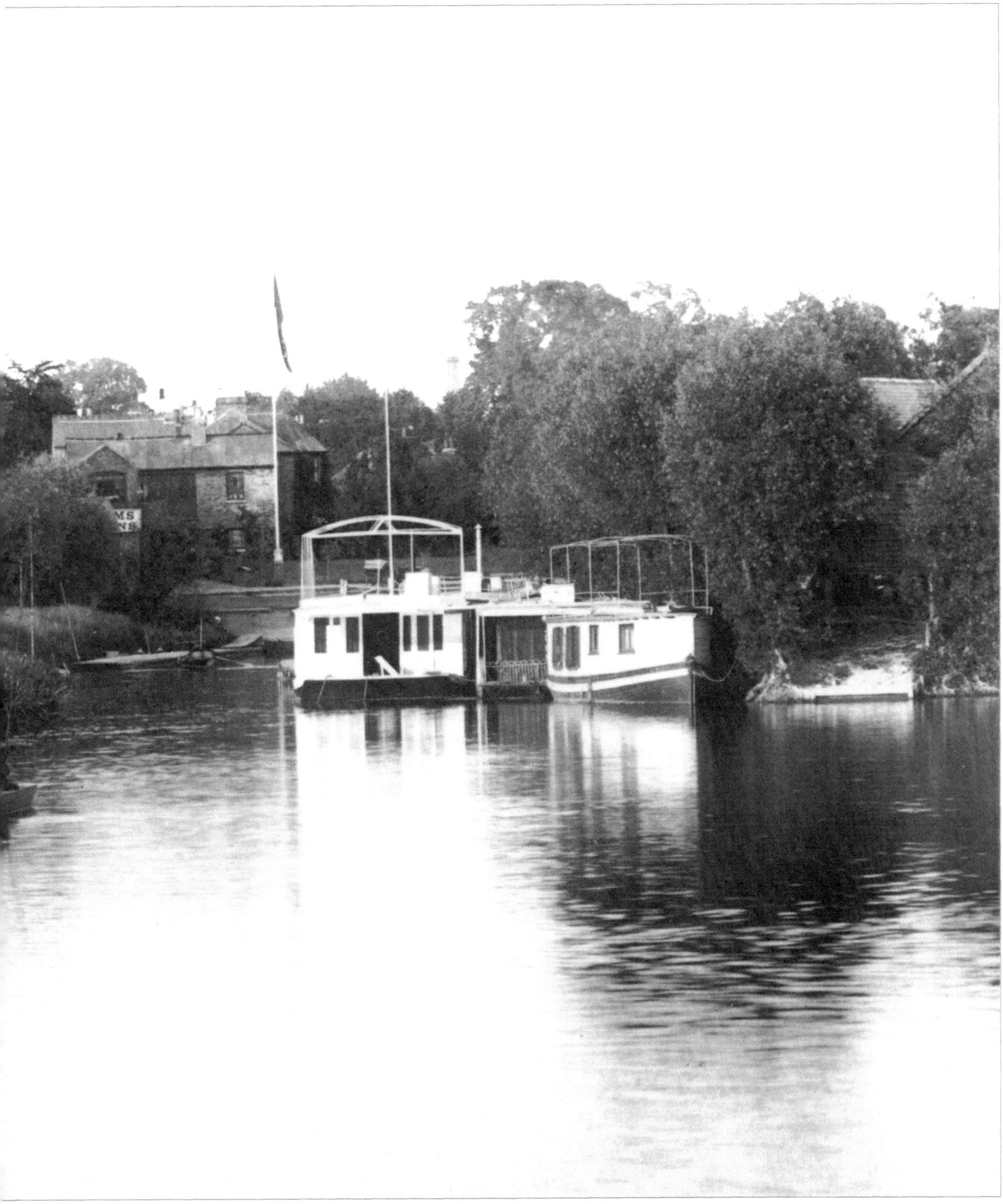

Did you know?

First Bus Service

Staines' first bus-service commenced in 1839. It was a daily return coach into London that departed from outside the Angel. The first motor-bus was a famously unreliable eight-seater service to Egham. A bus garage was built along London Road in 1936. It was one of the few Staines buildings to get the seal of approval from the art-historian Nikolaus Pevsner in his Buildings of England series.

Hooking On and Shooting Off

Here, behind the Packhorse, the towpath switches from one bank of the river to the other. Obviously this used to create problems for the horses that were towing the barges. If they were heading upstream, the horses were made to canter to this point, where they would be unhitched, and the barge would shoot off to the other bank under its own momentum. If heading downstream, the barge, freed from the horse on the Surrey side, would be carried over to the Packhorse by the current, and hooked onto the bank. The horses themselves would either make the crossing via Staines Bridge, or by the ferry that once operated here. The towpath is resumed at Egham Hythe.

The Towpath c1955 S175003

This complex process gives its name to the pair of cottages that are still sandwiched between the pub and the railway: they are called Hook On and Shoot Off.

Victorian Staines

River traffic had also taken a nose-dive. This was a shame, as Staines had never really managed to capitalise on its proximity to the Thames. The trouble was, too many people wanted the river for too many different things. The constant passage of commercial craft interfered with the fishing. In the past, riverside landowners had often diverted the current into their millraces (for there had been mills on the Thames, as well as on the smaller, faster rivers) and this sometimes left insufficient water in the main channel for boats to pass through safely. Tempers flared, and work failed to get done.

Numerous tempers were flaring around this time. The Chartist menace was abroad, and a lot of the population were shaking in their shoes. In 1825, Staines had formed its own militia. Originally 36 men strong, they were called out a couple of times in the disturbances of the 1830s. Later, during the Crimean War, they acted as a sort of Home Guard whilst the regulars were away. The Spelthorne Division Militia, of which Staines Militia was a part, was disbanded in 1854.

Hook On and Shoot Off in Thames Street 2004 S175710k (Russell Thompson)

Staines had been rather isolated by the first wave of railway-mania. The South-Western Railway went via Woking, the Great Western via Slough. In the 1840s, there was a flurry of proposals for railway lines that would include Staines. Not that the railway companies were particularly worried about Staines itself, they were vying to see who could reach Windsor first and Staines just happened to lie on some of the suggested routes. In fact, it was only Windsor's royal connections that kept these plans alive at a time when several other railway schemes were falling by the wayside due to lack of funds.

A line was built from Richmond to Windsor in 1848 by the Windsor, Staines & South-Western Railway. A small station was built at Knowle Green, half a mile east of Staines High Street. Staines was about to experience its first flush of popularity as a commuter town. It had the promise of fresh air and a stretch of river. Knowle Green was the first place to expand. It had previously been a thinly inhabited area of farms and cottages, but these were now being interspersed with villas and workmen's houses. Two railway-orientated pubs sprang-up on the corners of the station's approach-road, the North Star (named after a celebrated GWR engine) and the Railway Hotel.

With the railway, Staines gained the first of its iron railway bridges: this one, the aptly named Iron Bridge, straddles the eastern end

THE 1848 STATION-HOUSE 2004 S175711k (Russell Thompson)

of the High Street. It was originally a more curvilinear structure than we see today; 20th-century double-deckers found the arch difficult to negotiate and it had to be remodelled. In 1864, a second iron railway-bridge appeared, this time spanning the river just downstream of the Packhorse. It carried a new line that linked Staines with Wokingham. It is not one of the Thames' most attractive bridges (see 27255).

The railway had established itself quickly, but the road had one more trump-card to play. On 25 February 1871, Staines Bridge's toll-system was discontinued. The town was hung with flags and garlands and there were great scenes of rejoicing in the streets. In a final satisfying act the townspeople hauled the tollgate off its hinges and flung it into the water.

Along the road, Ashby's Brewery was still going strong. Staines began to attract some other big employers, including a candle factory and a lino-works. Firms realised that railway-links were essential for transporting their raw materials and finished products. The candle factory utilised an old farmhouse that stood on the corner of the London and Kingston Roads. The proprietor, W G Smith, bought the site in the 1860s. The house became his headquarters, and it incorporated a shop that sold the factory's produce. It also sold the soap

RAILWAY BRIDGE 1890 27255

that one of Smith's other businesses churned out. The candle 'manufactory' was always a conspicuous one in Staines, partly for its tall chimney, and partly for the ghastly smell that hung over it. This, combined with the aromas of the mustard mill and the brewery, helped to win the town the nickname of 'Smelly Staines'.

Less noxious was the smell produced by the lino-works. Frederick Walton had invented linoleum in Manchester in 1862, and arrived in Staines two years later. A hessian-backed mixture of resins, linseed oil and ground-up cork, it was the first hardwearing floor-covering within financial reach of ordinary people. At first Walton called it kampticon, before settling on the more euphonious name. What brought him to Staines was Hale Mill. Until recently it had been used as a calico-printing works and was equipped with a colossal pair of water-driven rollers that would be invaluable to the lino-making process. And Walton was grateful

STATUE IN THE HIGH STREET 2004
S175712k (Russell Thompson)

STATUE IN THE HIGH STREET 2004
S175727k (Russell Thompson)

Where Tilly's Lane meets the High Street there is a statue of two lino-workers in overalls, carrying a roll of their wares between them. Entitled Release Every Pattern, it was made by the sculptor David Annand

for the head-start, as it took a few years for lino to catch on. A number of people had faith in his invention, however, including Britain's Solicitor General who, with two other partners, pumped £30,000 into the venture. When lino did catch on, it did so in a big way: it became the favoured floor-covering of hospitals and shipping lines. Customers included Queen Victoria, who used it at Windsor Castle, albeit mainly in the stables. The works spread out, occupying the space immediately north of the High Street. Walton also purchased Pound Mill so the site now included both of Staines' ancient mills. By the end of the century it was to cover 20 acres. Terraces of employees' cottages were built in Hale Street and in Factory Path (now Mustard Mill Road, by the Iron Bridge).

The High Street itself was undergoing a metamorphosis. Initially a residential road, its houses were gradually being converted into shops, some of which were destined to become cornerstones of Staines. One of these was the business that would eventually be known as Johnson & Clark. It had been founded as long ago as 1790 by an ironmonger, Thomas Le Fevre. He leased the premises from one of the ubiquitous Ashbys. For years the shop occupied 19 High Street, next to the Blue Anchor. A Mr Johnson became involved in the 1870s, and the business went through a whole genealogy of names - Johnson & Linton, Johnson & Smith, Johnson & Sharp - before acquiring its best-known title in the early years of the 20th century. The shop would later expand and become synonymous with the Thames Street corner-site.

A PIECE OF STAINES LINOLEUM, SHOWING THE HESSIAN BACKING ZZZ00971

On the other corner stood a watchmaker's called Emary, which occupied the building with the clock in picture 35982. And next door to Emary's was another of Staines' Victorian institutions, Morford & Goodman, general draper, outfitter, milliner and dressmaker. It had been established here in 1849 by Robert Morford. He was a stalwart of the Congregational church in Thames Street, as was his later partner William Wreyford Goodman. The firm later diversified into sewing-machines and funeral regalia.

Another of the High Street's long-familiar names was that of Albert Willett, a blacksmith who gradually shifted into veterinary practice. In this latter role, the firm was occasionally called-upon by the royal family.

HIGH STREET 1895 35982

Dickens stayed at the Angel, which was then the Angel & Crown, and was yet to have its fine Georgian façade hidden by the perplexing mock-Elizabethan shell that it wears today. He allegedly based his Miss Havisham on the daughter of a local chemist. Lucky lady!

RUBBING FROM GORING GRAVE, ST MARY'S CHURCHYARD ZZZ00965

Willett's grandson was still working on the premises until 1964, after which his partner continued the business under a new name. The building, with its old carriage-entrance that had led to the forge, was swept away by the new Woolwich/Boots Opticians block that appeared in the late 1980s.

All in all, the High Street had seventy shops by the close of the 19th century. There were several grocers, cobblers, corn-chandlers and coal-merchants, plus one-off businesses such as a basketmaker, a carriage-builder, a pawnbroker and a monumental mason. Some of the long-vanished tradespeople have been fossilised in the form of street-names. Tilly's Lane is named after a family of bakers; Goring's Square after a butcher's shop. The Gorings had premises in the High Street from 1790 until the 1960s. Their shop latterly stood on the site that, for a while, was occupied by Tesco. You can still see early-Victorian Goring graves in St Mary's churchyard. In 1899 another butcher, Charles Reeves, built a handsome block of three shops on the north side of the High Street. The Post Office, which had been on the other side of the road, moved into one of them. It remained here until acquiring its present-day

HIGH STREET 1895 35986

The porticoed Westbourne House, on the right, was yet another Ashby residence. It was on this site that the butcher Charles Reeves erected his new block in 1899. The operation cost him £7,000; his neighbours thought he was mad.

THE OLD POLICE STATION 2004 S175713k (Russell Thompson)

This house at the corner of London and Kingston Roads was the police station from 1876 until the 1990s. It had previously been a one-storey building containing a dispensary. An earlier police-house, dating back to Bow Street Runners days, had stood on the opposite side of London Road.

Did you know?

Bricklayer Built His Own Cell

In 1880, the police station needed repair-work to its cells. A local bricklayer, one 'Socky' Bolton, was called in. Having completed the job, he blew his pay on a wild evening at the White Lion and was promptly arrested for being drunk and disorderly. He spent the night in one of his freshly built cells. One wonders if the mortar had even had time to dry.

home, east of the Garibaldi, in March 1931. Reeves' block is still there, a tall row with pointed gables, oriel windows and moulded brickwork, halfway between Tilly's Lane and Norris Road.

West of Thames Street, however, the High Street was in a state of decline. The removal of the old bridge had effectively rendered it a cul-de-sac. It was decided, at a meeting of the parish vestry, to demolish the old market-house which had been quietly collapsing for several decades, and replace it with something more in keeping with contemporary requirements. In 1880, work accordingly began on a new Town Hall. It was designed by John Johnson, and drew on elements of Flemish and Italianate architecture (see photograph 35979 below). He had recently completed a similar-looking building in Ipswich. Just below the clock-turret was an unofficial shield depicting two swans, a river and the London Stone. Staines was embarking on a period of civic pride. Down below, the stub of the old road was transformed into a new Market Square, and the market (which had been abolished in 1862) returned to the town.

THE UNPATENTED SEAL OF STAINES UDC
ZZZ00967

TOWN HALL 1895 35979

For all its more edifying features, it is often pointed-out that the Town Hall has a mistake on one of its clock-faces. Amongst its numerals, the figure XI is used twice, once as 11 and once as 9. The premises on the right are Ridley's timber-yard.

In 1894, the Local Board, which had administrated the old Spelthorne Hundred, turned into Staines Urban District Council and Staines Rural District Council. These were both housed in the new building. One of the UDC's first acts was to abolish the fairs that had been fetching-up in the High Street for longer than anybody could recall. Since 1816, the old four-day revels had become two separate one-day events: one on 11 May, dealing with horses and cattle, and one on 19 September for trinkets and vegetables. The latter became known as the Onion Fair, due to the 'large quantity of that esculent formerly brought for sale'. Proceedings also included a hiring-fair, where servants and casual workers were taken on.

A little later, the Urban District Council adopted the motto 'Ad Pontes Prospicimus' ('At the bridges we look forward'). But the Town Hall had in fact turned its back on one of Staines' major assets, the Thames. With the benefit of hindsight, several people feel that it set a precedent, and that most of the town's subsequent evolution has also ignored the river. It was not being ignored, however, by the cohorts of daytrippers who had suddenly discovered Staines. At weekends and public holidays, they flocked to the river with their picnics, trying their hand with whatever hired boats were available. A selection of boatyards were opened in order to meet the demand.

Local residents caught the fever, too, and set about forming various water-related clubs. These mainly catered for rowing and punting, but there was also a Staines Swimming Club that had its base on Church Island. Jerome

Boatyards

Tims' Boat-House 1895 35994

Victorian and Edwardian Staines was well supplied with boatyards and boat-houses. Mostly they were on the Egham side of the river. Above the bridge, on the former osier-bed, stood Taylor's and Biffen's yards. Further downstream, on either side of the Packhorse bridge, were Tims' (picture 35994) and Beedell's. Taylor's had a second yard on the Middlesex bank, next to the mouth of the Colne.

The boatyards built and hired-out punts, canoes and other small craft. Those yards that outlasted Staines' first wave of tourism soon found themselves letting out medium-sized motor-launches.

Biffen's survived until the latter years of the 20th century. By then, it was specialising in fibreglass cruisers, many of them for the overseas market. Its site was later developed as the Waterman's, a group of four large office-blocks.

Victorian Staines

BELL WEIR LOCK 1907 58000t

K Jerome waxed lyrical about Staines in his 1889 classic 'Three Men in a Boat'. His trio of protagonists, Harris, George and J (plus their dog Montmerency), weave past the town, negotiating locks and towpaths in their attempt to escape the rigours of metropolitan life.

As was mostly the case with Thameside resorts, Staines appealed to both the middle classes and the workers, and together they managed to cram the river almost solid between the Rennie bridge and the Packhorse bridge. The working classes, the so-called 'braces brigade', had been brought here by the railway and its comparatively cheap fares. The London & South-Western Railway were issuing posters that promoted Staines as

Bell Weir Lock is a mile upriver from Staines, and is now rendered slightly less peaceful by the proximity of the M25 bridge. But this was always a crossing-point of sorts - there used to be a ferry here.

THE TOWPATH NEAR ST PETER'S CHURCH 1890 23601x

68　STAINES – *a history and celebration of the town*

THE RIVER 1907 57993xp

Victorian Staines 69

BELL WEIR LOCK 1907 57999

being on a par with Henley and Marlow (see photograph 58000).

If Staines was to rival Henley, it was only proper that it should have its own regatta. At one point it actually had three. The first and longest-lived was the Staines Amateur Regatta, which was started in 1851. It is still held each July on the part of the river between Silvery Sands, the open space at the end of Riverside Drive, and the Packhorse railway-bridge (the stretch in photograph 23601x on pages 68-69).

Whilst this regatta was very much aimed at the well-to-do, the Staines & Egham Waterman's Regatta was more geared-up to the working classes. Founded in 1891, initially for vocational watermen, it had more of an emphasis on fun. Attractions included punting-races, and the river was lit-up after dark. This particular regatta came to a halt in 1930 - a time, perhaps, when the 'working classes' were becoming a less definable target-audience than had hitherto been the case. Another popular event that was discontinued around the same time was the Staines & Egham Juvenile Regatta. It took place on the neck of river between Church Island and the Lammas, a sheltered stretch that was safer for the young competitors. Spectators would cluster onto the banks of the Lammas. Again, there were light-hearted races, one of which, according to a contemporary report, involved a large cork crocodile that had been commissioned from the lino-works. All in

STAINES WEST STATION IN MOOR LANE 2004 S175714k (Russell Thompson)

all, it sounds like a precursor of the 1970s television programme 'It's a Knockout'.

As it happened, Staines was about to become even more accessible. For some time, a group of local businessmen and farmers had been agitating for another railway-line. They were concerned that Staines was not connected to the Great Western Railway or, more specifically, to the new catchment-area that it would open-up to their produce. It was also mooted that, with two railway companies operating from the town, prices might be kept to a competitive minimum. Unfortunately, the spirit of healthy competition also meant that the new project was not allowed to use the existing station, and as a result the two lines would not link-up.

Therefore, when the Staines & West Drayton Railway opened on 2 November 1885, it had a brand-new terminus. But it was not a new building (the budget had not allowed for that), it was a converted house. Previously known as Moor House, it had been home to Charles Finch, who owned the adjacent watermill. This was the ancient Pound Mill. Originally used to grind flour and grain, it was now specialising in mustard. Platforms were constructed in what had been Finch's front garden. The town's original station was rechristened 'Staines Junction', whilst the new one, considerably closer to the High Street, became simply 'Staines'. (In the 1920s, confusingly, they became 'Staines Central' and 'Staines West' respectively.)

In 1895, a halt was added at Yeoveney, to serve the soldiers going to and from a rifle range on Staines Moor. This installation, the Runnymede Range, was well equipped: it had a hundred targets, a clubhouse and a canteen. It replaced an earlier range, which had been closed in 1892 following complaints from the railway company: they considered it too close to their line and did not want any of their passengers to be accidentally shot. Although the Runnymede Range was abandoned by 1930, the halt continued to be used by local residents.

Heading north, the new, single-track railway cut across Staines Moor. Along with the Thames, this is Staines' foremost natural feature. In the 19th century, though, it was in a state of transition. From time immemorial, the Moor had been the domain of the 'commoners', those people whose houses bordered it and therefore had the right to graze their livestock on it. These rights were co-ordinated by a group of Moormasters, who were elected at the Lord of the Manor's sporadically-held court (known as the Court Leet). Everything changed in 1801, when the Act of General Enclosure was passed, giving landowners the right to section-off parcels of hitherto-public land for their own use. The threat in Staines came to a head in 1812-14. As in many other places there was an outcry and the commoners held rallies and drew up petitions. The residents of neighbouring Stanwell had actually marched on London when, in the previous century, similar threats had been directed at them. Staines, for the most part, won its fight. The infringement of commoners' rights was taken seriously once more, and compensation was often demanded: a plaque on a cottage in Moor Lane says it was built 'out of funds received for the extinguishment of Certain Common Rights'. And so, the Moor, Shortwood Common, Birch Green and other designated commonlands were saved for posterity. There were losses, however; the most bitterly-felt of which was when John Ashby, the last notable member of that clan, enclosed 15 acres of the Lammas.

Ashby and his fellow Quakers now had a new meeting-house, just to the south of the High Street. Its predecessor, along with the rest of Blackboy Lane, had been flattened by the Market Square development. This latest one, a handsome, colonnaded structure, had been built in 1844 by one Samuel Danvers, and had a burial-ground next to it. Prior to this, the sect had buried their deceased at the rear of Stainton House in Church Street.

One deceased Quaker was making a posthumous name for herself in the town's educational circles. Margaret Pope had herself been a teacher, having taught at the British School that had opened in Hale Street in 1808. (British Schools catered for the children of nonconformists, as opposed to National Schools, which were for churchgoing pupils.) Miss Pope's claim to historical fame is that her father, Robert, had been physician to George III: not a happy task, one imagines, though the doctor showed a degree of humanity that was seen as rather subversive at the time. (Robert Pope, incidentally, had shared his Staines practice with another Quaker, Dr Tothill, whose name long outlived him in the form of Tothill Street.) Margaret Pope founded her own school in 1831, and she left a trust fund to establish a new school after her death. The Margaret Pope School duly opened in Thames Street in 1874, and became something of a landmark with its little church-like spire.

Thames Street had, indeed, also been the site of a National School, though this moved to London Road in the 1860s. By the end of the century, there was an infants' school, too, in Wyatt Road, one of the little grid of new residential streets between the High Street and the railway. This building had been adapted from a former mission-hall that had itself been provided in answer to the town's growth. For, even in its enlarged form, St Mary's was proving inadequate for the booming population, hence the need for a succession of hastily erected church halls. The problem was addressed by Sir Edward

---

Did you know?

Kaiser Wilhelm's Window

There is a window in St Mary's Church that was donated by none other than the future Kaiser Wilhelm II. It is in memory of a Miss Augusta Byng, who lived in Binbury Row, just in front of the church. She had been nurse to the Kaiser's children on the occasions that, as a young man, he had stayed at Windsor Castle. He was, of course, Queen Victoria's grandson.

Victorian Staines 73

ST PETER'S CHURCH 1895 35996

ST PETER'S CHURCH COMMUNION TABLE 1895 36000

St Peter's sports an impressive array of fittings. As well as this carved wooden altar, there is a pulpit of brass and iron, and an unusual stone chancel-screen. The church was designed by G H Fellowes Prynne.

Clarke, the QC who had famously defended Oscar Wilde at his blasphemy trial. Tired of sitting through Sunday services in cramped buildings with no air-conditioning, he and his neighbours pitched-in and bought a plot of vacant building-land along Laleham Road. They felt it would be a good place for a new church. The result, St Peter's, opened its doors in 1894. An imposing example of the Gothic Revival style, it was one of Staines' few buildings to take advantage of its riverside setting (see photographs 35996 and 36000).

Three years later, Staines was indulging in nocturnal illuminations and celebratory dinners to mark Queen Victoria's Diamond Jubilee. Holgate's Wharf, south of the Packhorse bridge, was revamped as Jubilee Gardens. Not that Staines was unusual in any of these gestures. Victoria, however, had left her own little stamp on the town: the railway was given a new curve so that she could travel straight from Windsor to the Isle of Wight without changing trains. Perhaps it was feared that she would not be amused by Smelly Staines.

In order that the train could still stop in the town, though, a third station was built. This was Staines High Street station, which stood near the Garibaldi pub. It opened in 1884, although it was a short-lived venture, closing after only 32 years. By that time, of course, Victoria had been dead for more than a decade.

Victorian Staines

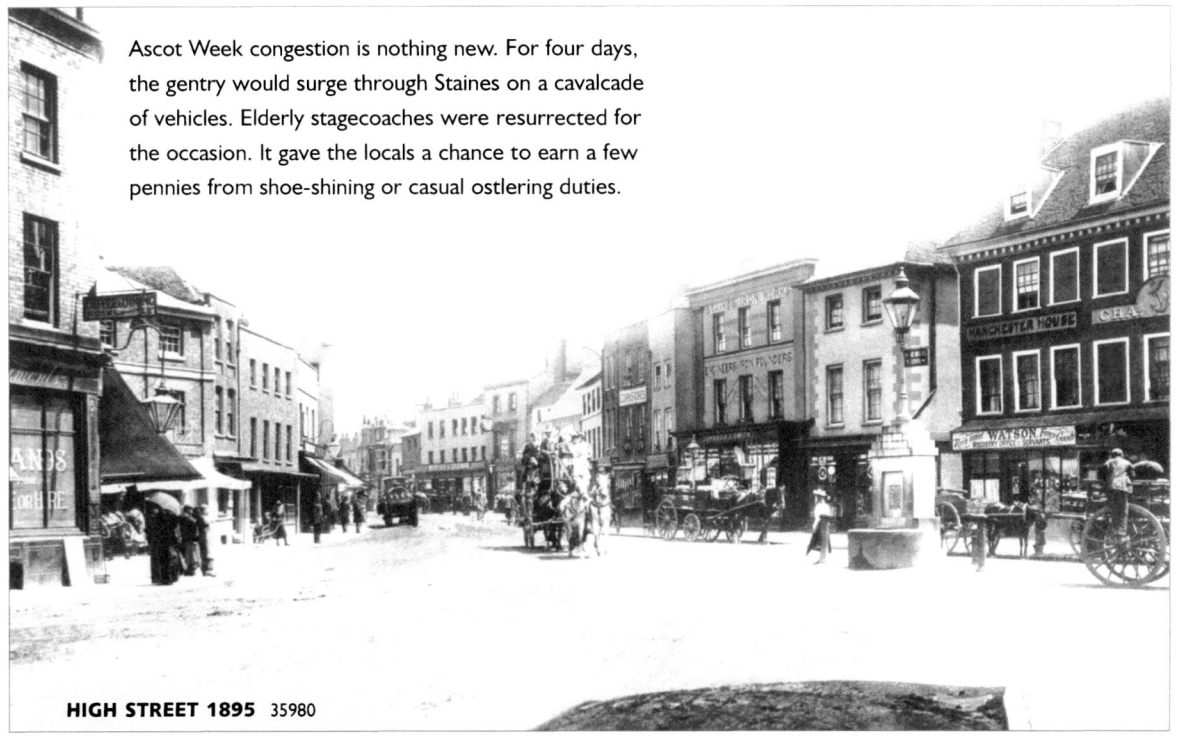

These shops are (left to right) G J Perkins, fruiterer-cum-butcher; Jeayes, Kasner & Co, coal merchants; J Goring & Son, butchers; and, with the white awnings, A Robinson, printer, and publisher of the West Middlesex Times. The contraption beside the fountain is a standpipe.

HIGH STREET 1895 35981

Ascot Week congestion is nothing new. For four days, the gentry would surge through Staines on a cavalcade of vehicles. Elderly stagecoaches were resurrected for the occasion. It gave the locals a chance to earn a few pennies from shoe-shining or casual ostlering duties.

HIGH STREET 1895 35980

STAINES ORDNANCE SURVEY MAP 1913

77

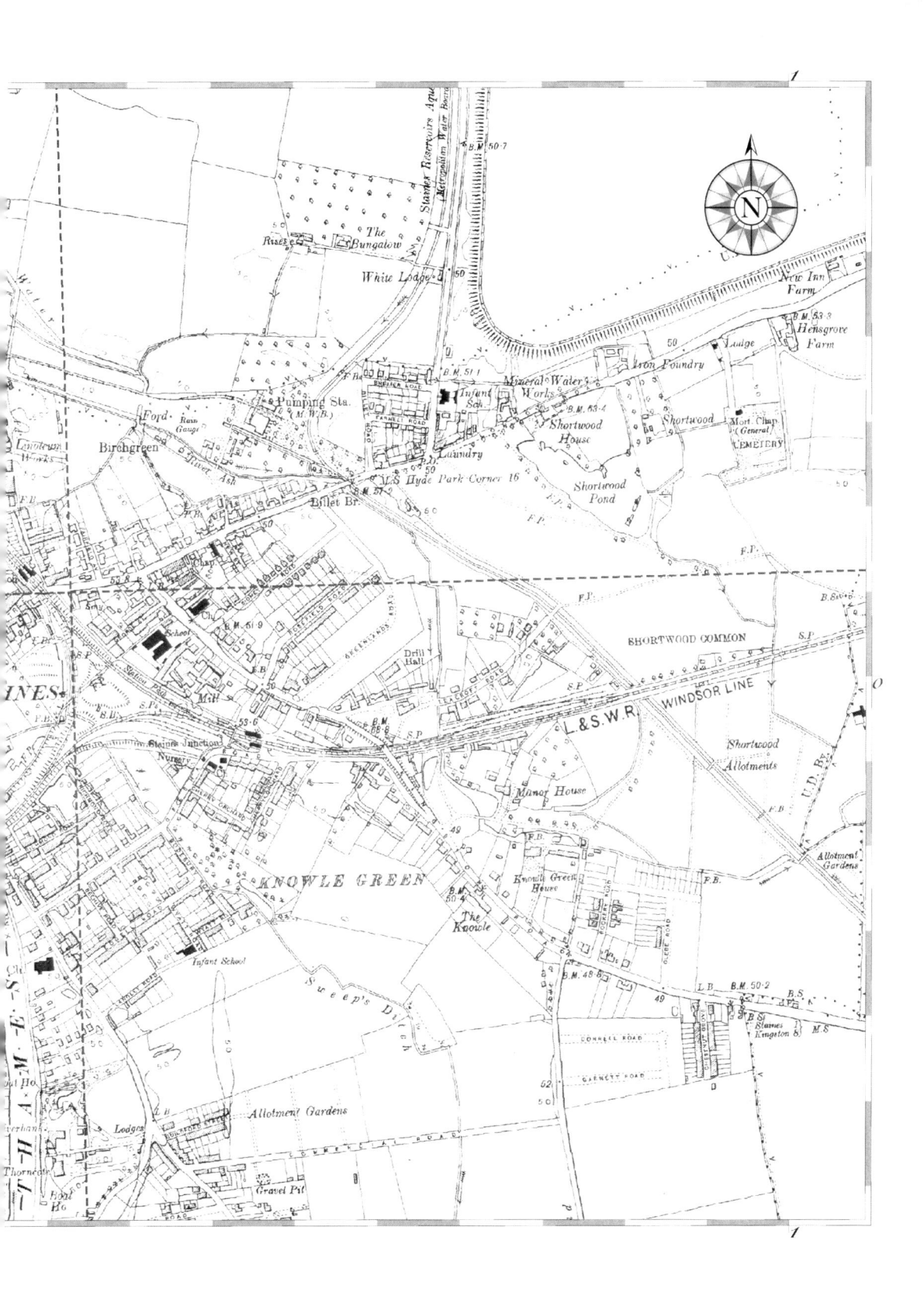

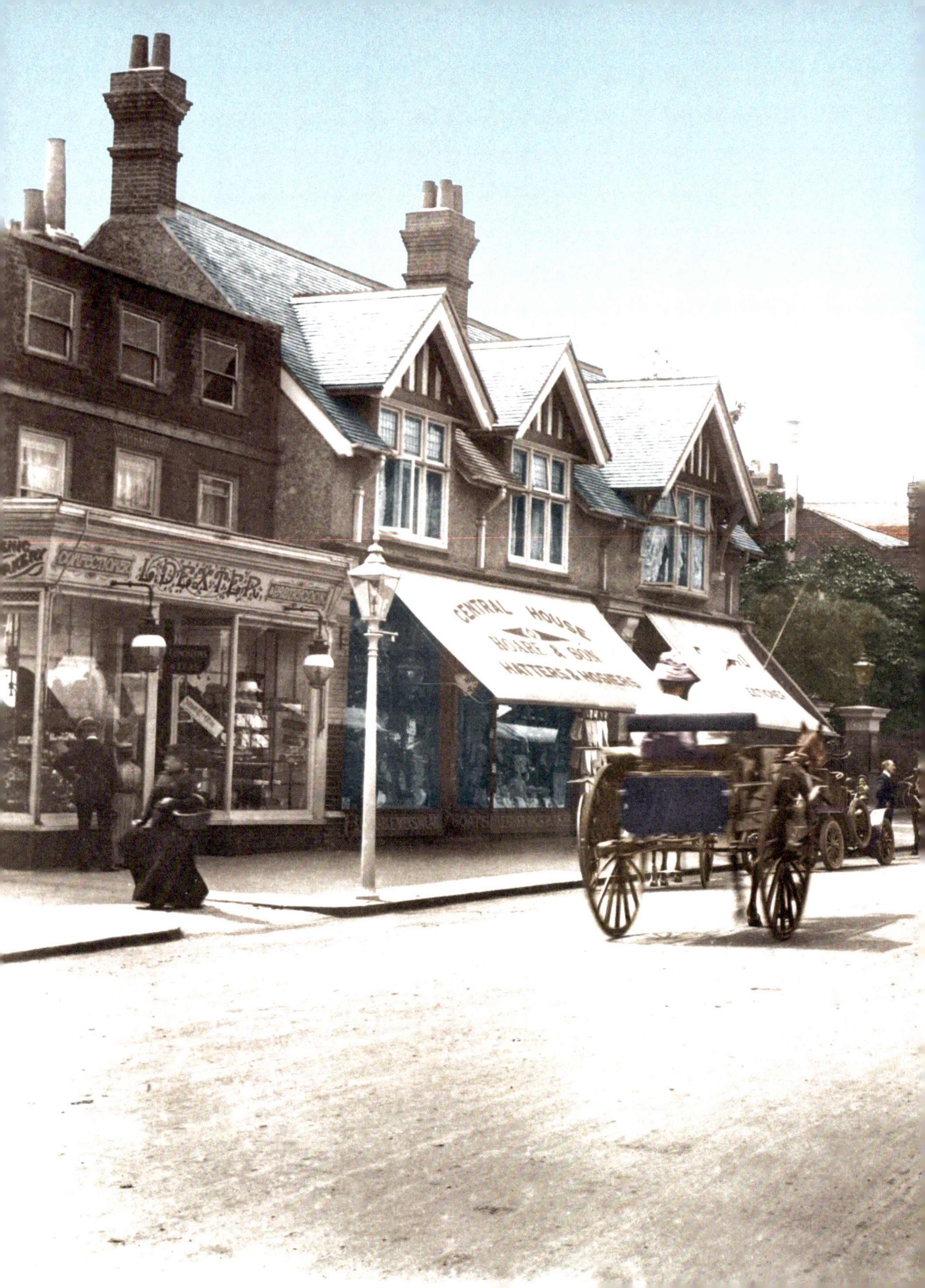
L. DEXTER
CENTRAL HOUSE
HOARE & SON
HATTERS & HOSIERS

CHAPTER FOUR

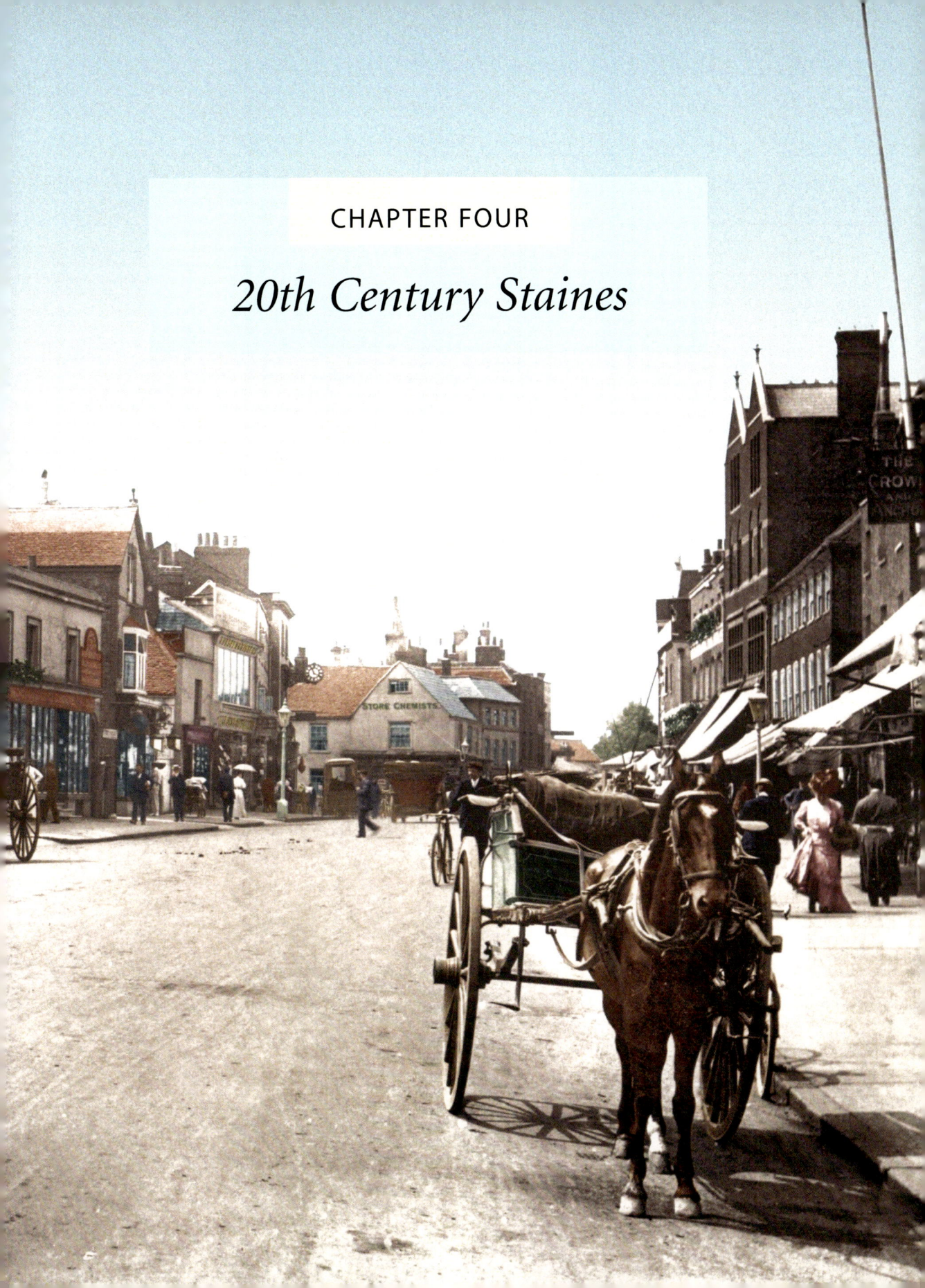

20th Century Staines

STAINES WAS growing apace. The 1801 population of 1,750 had mushroomed to more than 6,500 by the end of the century. It was set to grow much more, of course, not just in terms of the population, either, but in terms of the sheer size of some of its construction projects.

The first and most capacious of these was the Staines Reservoirs. Built between 1897 and 1902, just north of the London Road, the idea was that these two vast, back-to-back basins would supply water to London, but only in times of drought. In those days most water was drawn from rivers and wells. Standards change, of course, and processed water soon became the norm. Other reservoirs subsequently appeared in the surrounding area, though not as many as had originally been planned. All told, reservoir-building was an expensive business and in such a flat landscape the reservoirs had no natural valleys to nestle into, so all their embankments had to be specially built. There was another high price to pay, namely the loss of a large amount of farmland. Staines, at the turn of the century, was still largely agricultural and its chief products included cereal crops, beans and turnips. The town was proud of its non-urban aspects. Between 1900 and the 1920s, there was an annual parade of working horses, who were promenaded through the streets on Whit Monday morning.

The King George VI Reservoir, to the immediate west of the earlier pair, was to have its construction interrupted by the Second World War. Although it was finished by 1939,

HOUSEBOATS 1895 35993

it was not filled for another eight years. The MoD used it for various purposes.

But this was still in the future. In the years before the First World War, Staines' principal water-feature was still the River Thames.

The middle-classes rented holiday-homes here, or lived in ostentatious two-storey houseboats that they moored alongside Chertsey Lane. This stretch of the river became known as Houseboat Reach (see photograph 35993). By the 1920s, these same people were building chalets there, on the bank. Roads like Bundy's Way and Mayfield Gardens on the Surrey bank originated in this way. Many of these were simply holiday homes, although they had mostly mutated into permanent residences by the 1950s and 1960s. The working classes stuck to their punts (see photograph 57992), or caused occasional upset by leaping into the water 'improperly dressed'. Perhaps some of them remembered Staines' relatively clean water a few years later, when they found themselves waist-deep in Flanders mud. However, the fact was that the First World War did not only kill people, it killed entire ways of life, and the riverside was never as popular again. Some people have cited the widening horizons provided by the coming of the automobile; and also that, with increased holiday allowance, trippers no longer had to be mere daytrippers.

THE RIVER AND THE RAILWAY BRIDGE 1907 57992

Bridge House Hotel

Bridge House Hotel 1907 57994

Bridge House had been built in 1832, on land that was left over after the new bridge was built. It was later the home of the Finch family who ran the mustard mill. Tom Taylor bought it in 1898, and fitted-out the back garden as a boatyard. Space was limited, however, and he soon established a new yard next to Biffen's, on the other side of the river.

Taylor converted Bridge House itself into a hotel, with a special emphasis on the needs of London commuters. It was the first Staines residence to have electricity; it also possessed one of only two dancing-licences in the town (the other being at the Railway Hotel). Taylor sold it on in 1911, but subsequent proprietors ran into money-problems, and the hotel closed in 1937. Two years afterwards, the Regal cinema was built on the site.

Did you know?

Indian Prince

Thorncote, the home of Sir Edward and Lady Kathleen Clarke, was purchased in 1913 by the Indian cricketer Prince 'Ranji' Ranjitsinjhi. He changed its name to Jamnagar House. When the First World War broke out, he allowed the Red Cross to use it as a hospital, and he contributed £50,000 towards their costs. In 1924 he left Staines for Ireland. Jamnagar later became St Peter's vicarage.

POSTCARD FRONT 1907 ZZZ00960

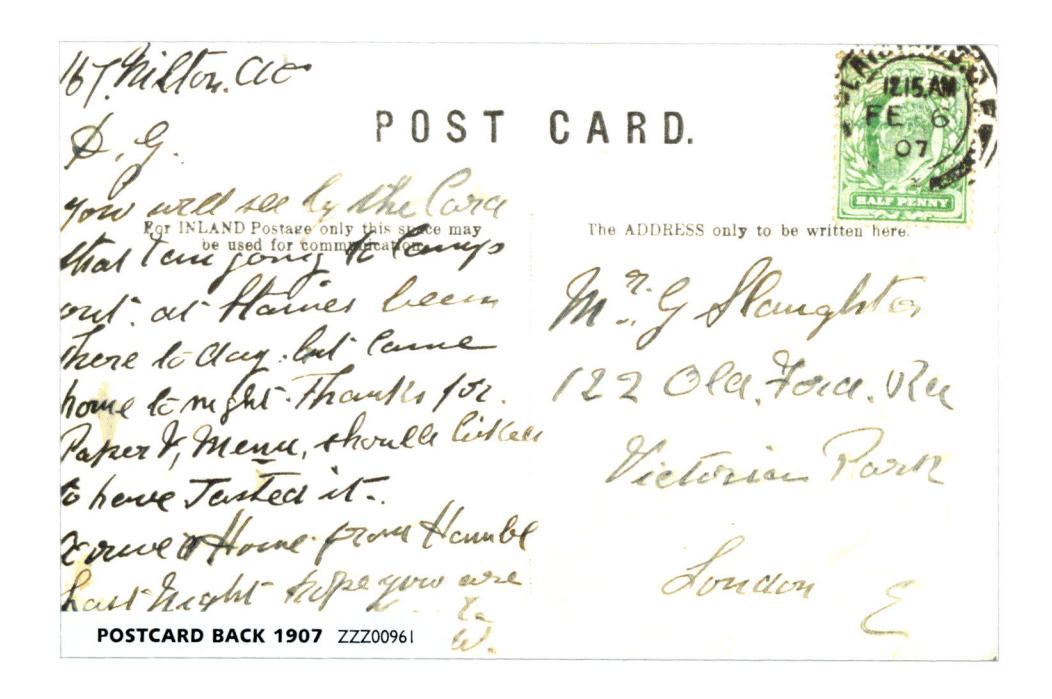

POSTCARD BACK 1907 ZZZ00961

20th Century Staines

POSTCARD FRONT 1914 ZZZ00962

POSTCARD BACK 1914 ZZZ0063

Two postcards from Staines' heyday as a riverside resort. The messages begin 'You will see by the card that I am going to camp out at Staines...' (1907), and 'My Dear Mother, just a card to let you know that we have arrived as far as Staines...' (1914).

The First World War claimed 198 Staines men. Their names are on a memorial erected in 1920 near the Town Hall. Almost half of them were lino-workers, though the fraction could have ended up being greater, as a total of 453 men from the factory had joined up. The memorial is supported by four figures, one at each corner, a soldier, sailor, airman and marine, and is surmounted by the Angel of Peace. The Town Hall Gardens, a popular public area between Market Square and the river, subsequently became known as the Memorial Gardens.

THE WAR MEMORIAL 2004 S175715k (Russell Thompson)

Whatever the ultimate reasons for the decline in its popularity, the riverside was no longer the only form of cheap entertainment in Staines. It was around this time that Staines had entered the cinematic age. The Margaret Pope School was converted into a cinema by the owner of a nearby photographic studio. It had closed to pupils in 1903, when the new Kingston Road School opened. In this new guise, the Palace, it kept going for about ten years. One reason for its closure was that there was now competition. A new picture-house, the Paris, had appeared in 1922. Later renamed the Empire, it boasted a fine interior of Art Deco plasterwork. Its closeness to the railway may have been a boon whilst Staines High Street station was still open, but it also meant that the screen quaked whenever a train passed by.

The Empire was, in turn, superseded by the Majestic. This stood on the other side of the Iron Bridge, just beyond the Garibaldi. Its only memorial now is in the name of a modern block called Majestic House. It was on the site of a building that had itself undergone a lengthy series of incarnations: this was originally a private residence called Fairfield House. In those days, this end of the town was considered rather select. Fairfield House later became a nunnery, and then a hotel-cum-restaurant called Marmaduke's. Then it changed hands and was renamed Sevens (or VIIs). The proprietor eventually left Staines and purchased a small island near Sark. The closure of Sevens caused a bit of local indignation, but its successor, the Majestic, also became a much-loved institution. It opened on 11 December 1929, with a showing of The Great Gabbo, an early Hollywood musical concerning the exploits of a self-obsessed ventriloquist. The Majestic's décor overshadowed even that of the Empire, an extravaganza of columns and panelling, it had a café painted to look like a Venetian courtyard. As such, the venue was a suitably atmospheric location for tea-dances and live concerts. By the time it closed in May 1961, it had become part of the Odeon chain.

Staines' fourth cinema, the Regal, was built in 1939 on the site of the old Bridge House Hotel in Clarence Street. Over the decades, it was divided several times into an increasingly complex multiscreen, and survived until the end of the century. Its chief claim to fame was that it had hosted the world première of Up Pompeii - not unfittingly, given that the extent of Staines' own Roman legacy was by then emerging.

Alternative forms of transport had also siphoned off the river's function as a commercial thoroughfare. The initial blow had been dealt, ironically, by the same railway that had brought the first influx of holidaymakers. Since 1857, the river had been in the hands of the Thames Conservancy, a twelve-person board composed of various City of London dignitaries, plus representatives from the Admiralty, Trinity House, and the Board of Trade. They rectified many of the Thames' traffic-flow problems by building locks and dredging the river-channel. Although the river still saw some commercial cargo as late as the 1930s, it was too late to reap the benefits.

ST PETER'S CHURCH 1895 35995p

As for the trippers, they had not entirely dried up. The car, indeed, was blamed for eroding some of the river's character.

Writing in 1939, the traveller Roland Wild observed that the Thames' visitors 'are in flannels and blazers, and its music is from a car wireless or a gramophone ... and its car-park attendants will crack a joke with you in London English and have given up posing as yokels'.

Laleham

Laleham, The Church 1890 27264

Laleham lies 2 miles downriver from Staines. All Saints' Church (picture 27264) is the burial-place of the poet and educationalist Matthew Arnold. His father was Dr Thomas Arnold, the famous headmaster who salvaged Rugby School from the moral laxity it had sunk into, and thus invented the concept of the Victorian public school as we know it. He taught at Laleham 1819-28. The church is largely Victorian, but has a brick tower of 1732.

Although Laleham is virtually joined to Staines by ribbon-development, there are 70 acres of open parkland to the south of the village. These were formerly the grounds of Laleham Abbey, a solid-looking exercise in classical architecture that was built for the Earl of Lucan in 1803-06. It is now divided into flats. The Lucans left their park for public use when they left the village in the 1930s.

20th Century Staines

The riverfront at Egham Hythe vaunts an unbroken row of late 18th- and early 19th-century architecture. Just upstream from the Swan are Riverside Bungalows, a line of once-ruinous cottages that were refurbished as summer-homes at the end of the Victorian era.

THE THAMES FROM THE BRIDGE c1960 S175020

Obviously keen to encourage Staines' leisure pursuits, John Ashby had given the Lammas back to the town in 1922. In the process, he amended its name to the John Ashby Recreation Ground. The townspeople, who felt he was giving them something that had always been theirs anyway, just carried on calling it the Lammas. (It was not until 1993, however, that this appellation became officially recognised again.) By the time he made this donation, Ashby was a long-standing JP, as well as being the Deputy Lieutenant of Middlesex and Chairman of Staines Urban District Council.

The Council, by this time, was in a state of flux. In the 1930s, Staines Rural District Council was abolished, in response to the growing urbanisation of the area. And, with Staines getting bigger and more multi-faceted all the time, the Urban District Council was outgrowing the Town Hall. They were soon seeking new premises. A suggested move into the old stable-block of Ashby's Brewery was vetoed on the grounds that it was slightly infra-dig. In the end, the various departments scattered to temporary offices around the town.

Although it no longer required its stabling, the brewery itself was in fine fettle. It already owned two hundred inns and beerhouses within a 30-mile radius. In 1903 it underwent a major rebuilding, gaining the tall tower that is still a familiar feature on the skyline today. The same year, Ashby's bought-out Harris' Brewery, a smaller venture based along the Kingston Road. By the end of the 1920s, Ashby's boasted all of the latest mechanical systems, and was able to greatly increase its supply of bottled beers. The firm was taken over in 1931 by H & G Simmonds of Reading. They in turn were later absorbed by Courage, and there was no more brewing at Staines after the 1950s. The bottling, too, ceased twenty years later.

Ashby's had also lost their bank to Barclay's in 1903. More than a century later, Barclay's still occupies the site. It is an early example of how high-street names began to proliferate at the expense of the smaller, localised firms.

The little gap, where the single-storey shops are, just seems to be crying out for the Elmsleigh Centre to be built. The cluster of tall buildings (with the chimneys) are all banks and incorporate the old Ashby's Bank premises seen in picture 35984.

HIGH STREET c1960 S175044p

One concern that remained very much Staines' own, however, was 'the Lino'. At its zenith, it had a workforce of 3,000 and was the size of a small village. It had its own gas-plant, fire-brigade, railway-sidings and sports ground. The last-named facility had an important social function for Staines, as the townspeople were encouraged to make use of it, especially for charitable events. It was often resorted-to on Thursday afternoons, as this was early-closing day. Staines Town Football Club played here in their Spartan League glory-years of the 1920s and 1930s. The ground was accessed via Mill Mead, next to the Iron Bridge.

The works served as a munitions factory during both World Wars, producing bombs in the First and torpedoes in the Second. Even in peace time, of course, the factory ran a serious risk of fire because of the nature of its raw materials. There was a particularly bad one in 1914. Eight miles of lino were apparently destroyed, although the firm was large enough to view it as little more than a temporary setback.

Ultimately less resilient was the candle factory. A fire broke out there at 9pm on 8 April 1924. Under the wrong circumstances, wax and fire are dangerous bedfellows, and it took three fire-brigades three hours and 400 gallons of water to contain the blaze. Afterwards, the wax had to be manually cut away. It had set 12 inches deep and solidified rivulets were still being extracted from nearby

LINOLEUM

A REGULAR weekly polishing keeps linoleum and waxcloths in very good condition, but through time the colours lose their brightness and look faded. Sour milk is very useful when this happens, and it should be applied with a rag that has first been soaked in turpentine. After rubbing the linoleum well, polish with a dry cloth. A good idea for getting a shine on linoleums and waxcloths without incurring the danger of slipping is to add a teacupful of paraffin to the water with which the floor covering is washed.

ADVICE ON LINO-CARE, FROM A HOUSEHOLD HINTS BOOK, 1937 ZZZ00975

A 1934 LAGONDA SALOON, AS DEPICTED ON A BROOKE BOND TEA CARD ZZZ00969

drains as late as the 1960s. The remaining buildings were demolished, and that was the end of candle-making in Staines.

After linoleum, Staines' biggest export must have been its Lagonda cars. This firm originated in the back garden of a house along Thorpe Road, not far from Egham Hythe. It was started by Wilbur Gunn, who was simply setting out to build a steam-yacht and a type of motorbike. By 1906, however, he had made his first car, and was soon operating under the name Lagonda. He was an Ohio man and took the name from a river near his hometown. A large factory grew on the site of Gunn's house, where Sainsbury's now stands. For a while, the cars were hugely successful. A Lagonda won the Le Mans 24-hour race in 1935, but thereafter, the firm was beset by economic difficulties. Lagonda left Staines in 1947, and the factory, with its fine 1930s façade, was taken over by Petters, a West Country firm who made diesel engines. Petters, at their peak, became the biggest employer in the district.

Despite the aforementioned hazards at some of the factories, Staines was not really equipped to deal with human catastrophe on a large scale. However, there was now a Cottage Hospital along the Kingston Road. This opened in May 1914. Lady Kathleen Clarke (Sir Edward's wife) had no sooner performed the ceremony, holding aloft a specially-made golden key, than the first patient was rushed in. It was, indeed, to be a busy little hospital, and was a source of pride for the local populace, who organised regular fundraising activities for it. Some of its thunder was stolen in 1939 with the opening of Ashford Hospital (although this was not strictly a new establishment, having started life in 1840 as the Staines Union Workhouse). Staines Hospital - it had dropped the Cottage - continued as a general hospital until the 1960s, though by the early 1980s it was just an administrative centre. The building was pulled down in 1985.

As early as the 1930s, sadly, a high proportion of the hospital's patients were the victims of road accidents. It dealt with 139 cases in 1933 alone. Traffic, in general, was becoming a problem in Staines, not least from the point of view that the town was a major bottleneck at holiday weekends. The banner that once hung on the Iron Bridge saying 'Gateway to the West' was often greeted with a mirthless chuckle. Plans were already being drawn-up for a bypass between the Crooked Billet, a once-remote pub on the London Road, and the Glanty at Egham. Because of the Second World War, the road did not materialise until 1964.

The Second World War did more than interrupt roadworks. Lagonda and the Lino turned their hand to munitions. So did the top floor of Perrings furniture-shop in the High Street (the site is now Peacocks), where an all-female production-line turned out armature-coils for explosive devices. The RAF tested its new bouncing bombs on the Staines Reservoirs. Staines was itself hit by several bombs, the worst raids occurring during 1944. The town was fortunate in that much of its acreage - the Moor and the other common lands - was sparsely inhabited. Four people were killed one night in Stainash Avenue, but otherwise Staines was relatively lucky. Kingston Road School also sustained bomb-damage, and its older pupils were temporarily taught in the half-built Matthew Arnold School (whose completion had been delayed by the outbreak of the war, and was not properly opened until 1954). Measures had been taken in 1939 to safeguard the local transport network. A link was finally laid between the town's two railway-lines, and a temporary bridge was built, just to the west of the Rennie bridge. This creation, made by the firm Callender Hamilton, would provide a secondary crossing if the other bridge was bombed and it would also help to shoulder the weight of the anticipated military traffic. The bridge became pedestrian-only in 1947, and was completely dismantled twelve years later.

Did you know?

Persistent Myth

There is a curiously persistent myth that, during the Second World War, a replica of Clapham Junction station was fashioned inside the still-empty bowl of the King George VI Reservoir. This was supposedly a decoy for enemy bombers. It would have been a foolhardy place to lure bombers to, however, with Feltham's vital marshalling-yards not far away. The reservoir is not open to the public, hence, perhaps, its mystique.

THE RIVER AND THE TOWPATH c1960 S175036

In 1947, Staines experienced a natural disaster, though it was not one that resulted in any loss of life. That March saw the heaviest rainfall for more than a century. The ground was still frozen from what had been a bad winter, and was therefore unable to soak-up the water. The equivalent of three months' rain poured into the Thames at once, and the river rose more than 6ft above its normal level. Obviously this was much too much, and large areas of the Thames Valley were flooded. Stanwell, Ashford, Shepperton and Sunbury were badly affected; Egham Hythe was awash. In Staines the worst-hit areas were Moor Lane, Wraysbury Road and Kingston Road. The danger was as much posed by seemingly insignificant tributaries as by the Thames itself, and the problem was exacerbated by strong winds. Residents were evacuated and given shelter in the Town Hall and Duncroft. When the waters had abated, the Council issued free disinfectant, and unrationed soap temporarily hit the shelves. The affair caused £10,000-worth of damage. To add insult to injury, the rest of the year was absurdly dry and hot. There was even a drought in August.

By then, Staines was in the mood for more civil engineering. Various road-widening measures were implemented in the town, the most notable of which once again involved the top end of Thames Street. Johnson &

HIGH STREET 1907 57995p

Clark, the ironmongers, had expanded their premises to include the corner of the street, and in 1956 they built a new store on the site. It was an ambitious move, as they were now reinventing themselves as a department store. On the opposite corner stood Kennards, an extended version of the shop that had once been Morford & Goodman (it ended up occupying the block on the right in photograph 57995). One casualty of the Thames Street work was the Congregational church, an imposing early Victorian building with Ionic columns and a portico.

Another sorely-missed victim of road-widening was the White Lion, a fine Elizabethan pub that stood between Marks & Spencer and the Iron Bridge. We know its vintage from a 16th-century coin that was discovered under the floorboards. By the end of the 19th century, one of its rooms was doubling as the courtroom for the local petty sessions. The pub even had its own iron-barred lock-up. Although it was a listed building, it supposedly projected too far into the High Street, and was therefore another landmark to be demolished in 1956.

Along the road stood Dexter's Café, a popular local rendezvous. It was where the HSBC Bank now stands. Lewis Dexter had begun as apprentice baker in Church Street, but had graduated to his own High Street premises in the early years of the 20th century (see photograph 57997). He added the café, a few doors along, in 1927.

Less lamented is the notorious gasholder. Its vast bulk tended to prejudice some of Staines' visitors, amongst them the writer S P B Mais, who described the town as 'an unsightly medley of gasworks and reservoirs from which it is pleasant to turn aside' ('The Home Counties', 1942). Like most things in Staines, gas had primarily come here because of the bridge. A year after it was built, its fourteen lamps were being lit by gas. This was supplied by the Staines & Egham Gas and Coke Company, which stood along the Causeway. The gasholder, all 177 ft of it, when holding its full quota, was built in 1927-28. There is a story that, in the early days of Heathrow Airport, an arrow was painted on the gasholder's circular top, in order to direct the pilots towards the runways. The only problem was that, as they rise or sink, gasholders rotate! This one was dismantled in 1985-86.

If writers did not mention the gasworks, they usually alluded to the level of congestion in the town. It was inevitable that Staines would be congested as it was still expanding rapidly. There had been another spate of new housing in the 1930s, spawning developments such as the Victoria Park estate off Kingston Road. A few miles to the north, a somewhat larger engineering programme was afoot. The Great West Aerodrome had been in operation since 1930, as an alternative to the frequently waterlogged one at Northolt. In 1946, it ran its first scheduled flight as London's new airport. It is what we now call Heathrow, and has been responsible for some of the local population-growth, particularly at Stanwell, Lord Knyvett's old stomping-ground.

Before the coming of Heathrow, Yeoveney had been considered a potential airport-site. Obviously this would have amounted to an ecological catastrophe for Staines Moor, but then, the Moor seemed to be perpetually faced with some sort of danger. In 1968, the manor was inherited by a Mrs Galbraith, who made moves to start extracting gravel from the Moor. Since it was her property, she could theoretically do what she liked. And, indeed, gravel-digging is permitted on certain parts of the Moor. Once again, however, it was felt that the commoners' rights were being called into question, and her application was overturned. She sold the Lordship to the chairman of a sand and ballast company, though - just in case.

Another site that finally vanished beneath gravel-workings was Staines Stadium in Wraysbury Road. It seems curiously forgotten now, but during the late 1940s and the 1950s, it was a well-attended venue for greyhound-races and stock-car events. It had all the requisites - terracing, grandstands and floodlights - but half the site had to be levelled in the early 1960s for Staines Bypass. The diggers did the rest.

The last quarter of the 20th century was a time of transition for Staines. It is hard for an industrial town when the demand for its goods dries up. The Lino was hit hard by the advent of vinyl floor-coverings. Between the wars, the firm had merged with a Kirkcaldy company, Barry, Ostlere & Shepherd, to become the Barry (Staines) Group and, following a period of decline, much of the equipment was transferred to Scotland. The bulk of the buildings were pulled down in 1973, or thereabouts. Linoleum was now chiefly the preserve of art-students and printmakers, who were unlikely to be ordering it in the volume that the White Star shipping line once had.

The Quakers moved on, too. In 1975, the local membership was amalgamated with that of Egham. The fine Victorian meeting-house had been demolished in 1936, and the burial-ground discontinued eight years later. Fittingly, the final interment had been the body of one Charles Ashby. The family had just about fizzled-out in Staines. Charles, however, was not to rest undisturbed, for the site came within the bounds of a scheme to redevelop the area south of the High Street. At least this provided an opportunity to excavate the site, just as soon as the human remains had been removed and reinterred.

The importance of Roman Staines had scarcely been guessed-at until 1969, when the archaeologist Maureen Rendall directed a dig at the nearby Barclay's Bank site. The work continued in 1974, after the demolition of Elmsleigh House, a large late-Victorian residence just to the east of the burial-ground. Originally home to yet more Ashbys, it had for the last two decades of its life housed the Clerk's Department of Staines UDC (see photograph 57997 on page 104). Both Elmsleigh House and the burial-ground threw up plentiful evidence of Roman occupation.

Although its site is obliterated, Elmsleigh House gave its name to the Elmsleigh Centre, the ambitious shopping precinct that was officially opened in February 1980. The centre was part of a major scheme to develop South Street, which had existed

HIGH STREET 1907 57997x

Did you know?

The Golden Boy

Attached to the frontage of Dexter's Café was a gilded figurine known colloquially as 'the Golden Boy'. Its proper name was the Daughter of the Goddess of Fame. It is believed to have started life as the emblem of a paint company. When the café was demolished in 1986, the figure was re-homed in various public places until its eventual theft (see photograph 35984, page 39).

The Crown & Anchor, its sign visible on the right, was another pub that bit the dust in the late 1950s. It was apparently of 17th-century origins, but the brewers claimed that it was 'only' Victorian when they were seeking permission to pull it down.

as a stretch of one-way system since 1974. This new road triggered another phase of redevelopment. A new library appeared, and the row of buildings in Thames Street, between Debenhams and Tothill Street, was demolished. This block included several small shops, as well as the old Margaret Pope School.

There were bigger road-building projects also waiting in the wings: in 1985, the Staines section of the M25 opened, sweeping to within a mile of the town. For a short distance, it used the route of the Staines & West Drayton Railway. This had ceased active passenger-service in March 1965, although the locally-based Cory's Oil Depot was still using it as a freight-line into the early 1980s. Staines West station-house stood forlornly for a few years before being sold to the Council for the princely sum of £1. It was

Stanwell

Stanwell, The Village Hall c1955 S588029

Stanwell is a sea of modern development with, at its core, a triangular medieval green. There are a smattering of 18th- and 19th-century houses. Two pubs in the High Street, the Bell and the Swan, were here by at least 1730. Stanwell's oldest building, though, is St Mary's Church, which retains some 13th-century details. The building has a well-known leaning spire.

Lord Knyvett founded a school here in 1624. The inscription over its doorway, 'Train up a child in the way he should go, and when he is old he will not depart from it,' is fitting, for it is now an adult education centre.
Stanwell has two artificial rivers, which run in parallel drains past Heathrow's cargo terminal. The Duke of Northumberland's River was built to drive a 15th-century flour-mill at Twickenham; the Longford to feed the water-features at Hampton Court.

subsequently converted into offices and now houses Orchid Graphics. The other station, Staines Central, had quietly changed its name back to 'Staines', now that its old rival was being put out to grass.

Staines Bridge, just along the road, had far fewer upheavals in the 20th century than it did in the 19th. Compared with the non-stop problems encountered by its two predecessors, the Rennies' bridge had required a negligible amount of structural repair-work. The family's engineering skill seems all the more impressive when one considers the enormous changes in the nature of vehicular traffic since the bridge was built. The Rennies initially recommended a weight-limit of 'not to exceed 10 tons' for their new construction. This is obviously a drop in the ocean compared to the weights it routinely carries today. And yet, apart from repairs in 1910 and 1993, it has needed no major attention. If the bridge had a fault, it was that it had always been rather narrow. Overhanging pavements were added in 1958 to try and remedy this. The workmen buried some old Second World War shell-cases under the footpaths to act as counterweights. These caused some consternation when they were dug up during the 1993 renovations, as their function had long been forgotten and it was feared that they might still be live. As it happened, the bridge did still have its wartime demolition charges in situ, and these had to be carefully defused.

Like the road and the railway, the river was also having to adapt to new ways. After the Second World War, it became alive once again with houseboats, though this time the owners were people who were otherwise homeless, rather than the Charleston-dancing weekenders. Until petrol came off ration, most of these craft had to be manually driven. Thereafter came the

HIGH STREET c1960 S175045

outboard motors and the Thames was once more a boatpersons' playground. Penton Hook Marina, 1½ miles downstream on a hairpin kink in the river, opened in 1960, with moorings for 625 vessels (see photograph S175052).

With Heathrow constantly expanding, air-traffic was also on the increase. And, one grey afternoon in 1972, Staines was visited by a disaster that has never been forgotten. At 5.11pm on 18 June, a British European Airways jet, which had taken off from Heathrow only three minutes before, crashed at the edge of the town. None of the 118 occupants survived. The only faint blessing was that nobody on the ground was also killed, because the plane had fallen near the Lino's sports-field, only a whisker away from the High Street and the Crooked Billet roundabout. The fact that these roads were clogged with holidaymakers rather hampered the rescue operation. The plane burst into flames soon after the emergency services arrived, after which the roads became further congested by onlookers. An investigation concluded that the airliner's wing-droops had been locked when they should have been unlocked. The incident remains one of Britain's worst air-disasters. A memorial to the victims was unveiled 32 years later, on 18 June 2004, after a special service at St Mary's Church.

It was indeed a new era. Since the Council's departments had been redistributed around the town, the Town Hall had lived through a series of different functions. It staged plays and boxing-tournaments, and in the 1960s

Staines jet crash memorial

A MEMORIAL to one of Britain's worst air disasters is being unveiled in Staines today. When a Trident airliner crashed 100 yards from the Staines by-pass exactly 32 years ago, 118 people died. The passenger jet crashed just after take-off from Heathrow.

LONDON EVENING STANDARD EXTRACT 2004 ZZZ00974

became a popular venue for rock gigs. Bands such as the Who and the Yardbirds played there. It survived a threat to demolish it in the 1970s. When the councillors put its future to the ballot, it was spared by a single vote. But its future was still far from secure. In 1982, it provided the setting for the courtroom scenes in the film Gandhi, although the set-designers had rendered it virtually unrecognisable.

In 1993, the Town Hall opened as an Arts Centre. At the same time, the London Stone was placed inside. For the past seven years it had lived in Staines library, having been rescued from a swathe of undergrowth at the Lammas. The Stone celebrated its 800th birthday in 1997, the festivities being presided-over by the current Lord Mayor of London. Moves are currently afoot to return it to the library again. Sadly, the Arts Centre scheme was not as successful as might have been hoped, and it had closed again by the end of the decade. Come the new millennium, there were applications to turn the Town Hall into a bar - applications which, unsurprisingly, were hotly contested by local residents and thrown out. Uncertainty still looms over it.

102 STAINES – *a history and celebration of the town*

PENTON HOOK LOCK c1960 S175052

20th Century Staines

Lewis Dexter's bakery is on the left. To the right, amongst the foliage, is the entrance to Elmsleigh House.

HIGH STREET 1907 57997

THE ELMSLEIGH CENTRE: UNDERGOING RENOVATIONS IN 2004 S175716k (Russell Thompson)

Since 1965, when the county of Middlesex vanished in a puff of bureaucratic smoke, Staines had been part of Surrey. There had even been talk of annexing it to Greater London. The Urban District Council itself moved in 1972 to a massive cathedral-like complex at Knowle Green. Two years later, Staines UDC was conjoined with that of Sunbury to form the Borough of Spelthorne. The two towns were fiercely independent, and it initially felt like a marriage made through gritted teeth. The civic heralds tactfully designed the new borough a coat of arms that incorporated elements from the shields of both parties - Staines' bridge and Sunbury's sunburst - along with a motto that similarly combined the two former mottoes. So 'Ad Pontes Prospicimus' and 'Sol et Pastor Deus' became 'Ad Solem Prospicimus' - 'We Look Forward to the Sun'. There was, indeed, a whole new millennium on the horizon.

20th Century Staines

THE RIVER 1907 57989x

SPELTHORNE BOROUGH COUNCIL OFFICES AT KNOWLE GREEN 2004 S175717k (Russell Thompson)

PENTON HOOK LOCK c1960 S175052

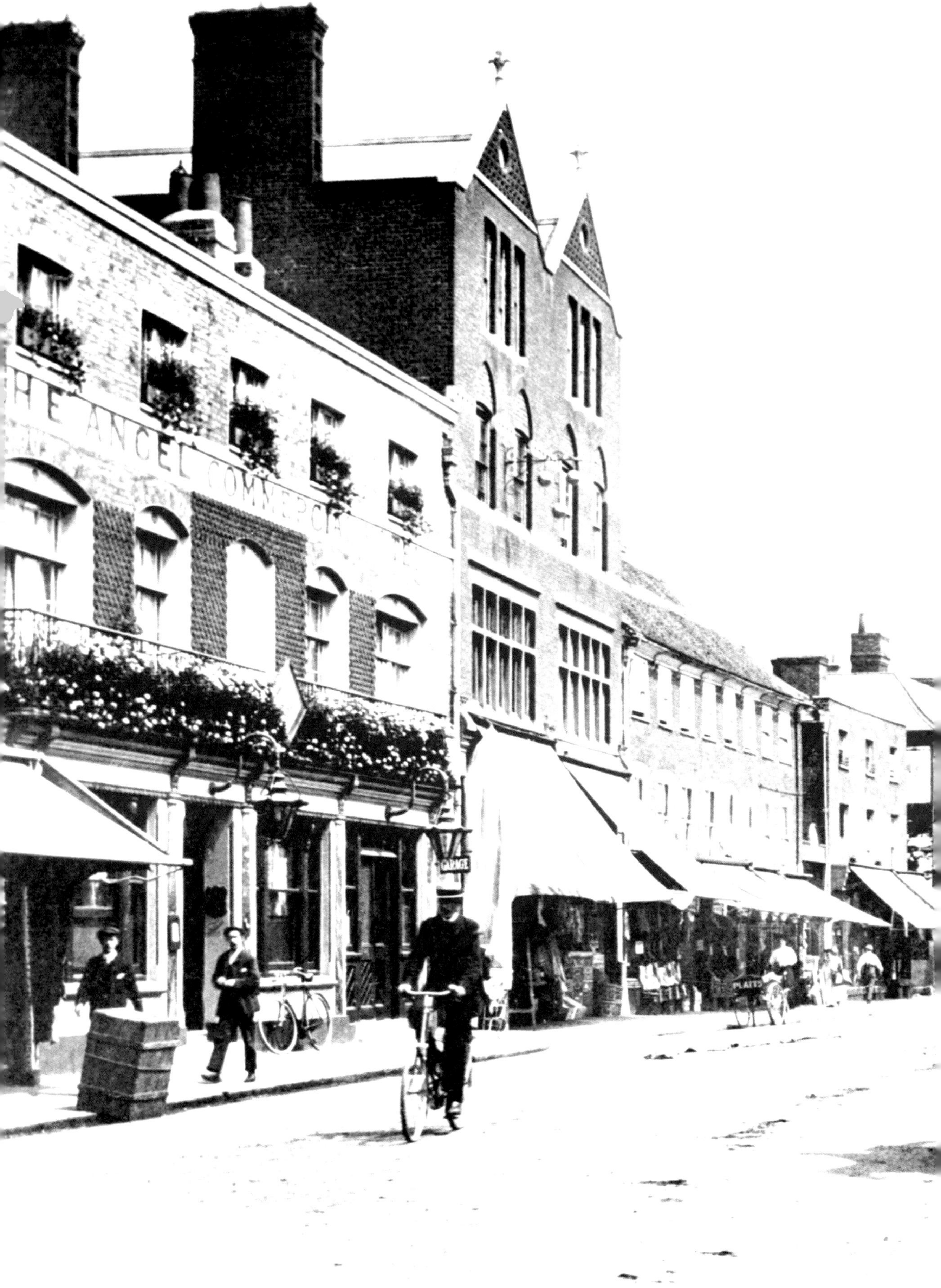
GARAGE

HIGH STREET 1907 57995p

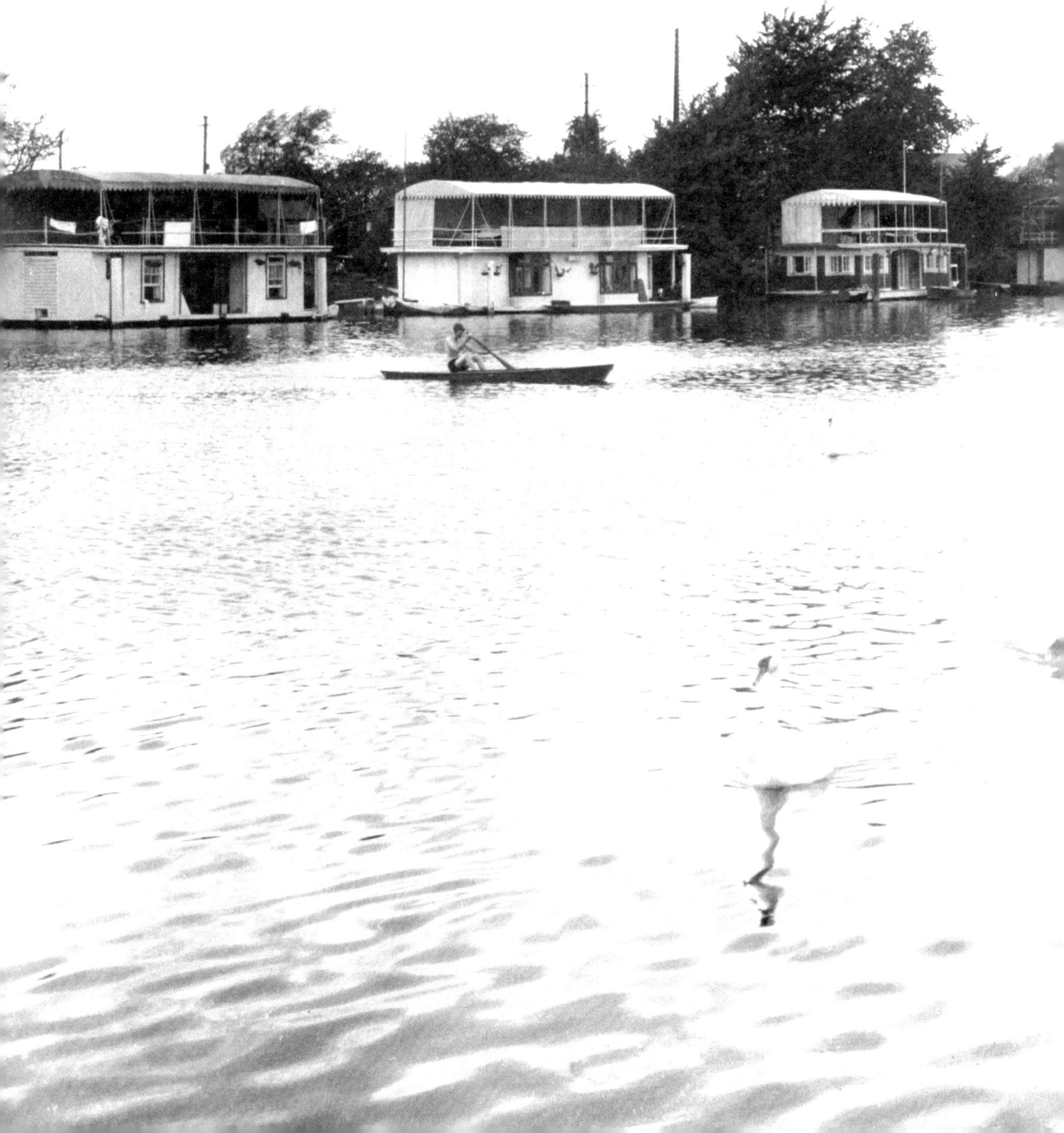

CHAPTER FIVE

Looking Forward

TAKE A look at Staines High Street. Walk from the Iron Bridge to the Town Hall, taking in not just the shop fronts themselves, but also the buildings that contain them. What you will see is not exactly a glowing example of uniformity - some people might call it a hotch-potch - but it is an excellent cross section through the town's history. The 1899 post office block now contains a building society and a shop where you can buy takeaway caffe lattes. The Angel still has its old name high up on its façade, but it is now a chic 21st-century bar. Art Deco rubs shoulders with mock-Elizabethan and

Egham

Egham, High Street c1955 E27053

Having crossed the Thames at Staines, the Roman road passed through Egham on its relentless way to Silchester. The Saxon settlement, 'Ecga's farmstead', had become a little town by the time of the Norman Conquest.

Its 11th-century church was replaced in 1817-20 by the present nonconformist-styled building. Amongst the treasures inherited from the older church is a wall-monument to the 17th-century judge Sir John Denham, showing the dead man wearing his shroud like a head-dress as he rises from a gaggle of jostling skeletons. Sir John's son, also John, was a poet; his best-known work, 'Cooper's Hill', celebrates the Egham landscape.

Egham's former Literary Institute now houses, amongst other things, an excellent little museum. Staffed by a team of knowledgeable and committed volunteers, it is well worth a visit.

buildings that have '2001' inscribed on them. It is like looking at geological strata. In one glance we can take in the ancient and the bang-up-to-date. We have seen that Staines' history has concerned itself with reinvention. It is a natural, ongoing process.

So how does a town celebrate its past whilst manoeuvring itself into an age of new trends and new ways of thinking? Very often, the two things are mutually exclusive, and the balance is hard to get right. People cannot live in museums. Certain kinds of buildings, for instance, simply become redundant. And then there are the issues created by traffic: sometimes the importance of road-widening, as we have seen, outweighs the importance of whatever unfortunate edifice is jutting out into the roadway. But Staines, on the whole, is good at preserving its past, which is particularly impressive when one considers that a lot of its recent developments have been on an ambitious scale.

Between 1997 and 1999, the Two Rivers retail park was built. Taking its name from the Colne and the Wraysbury, which border it and cut through it, the site was virtually a hallowed ground, as it was where 'the Lino' had once stood. The factory had given way to the Central Trading Estate. The present development was designed with 21st-century trading in mind, combining a string of high-street names with a new cinema, a variety of eating-places and extensive car-parking.

Two Rivers is, of course, Staines' third shopping-area, alongside the Elmsleigh Centre and the High Street. But it is not just about big names, and there are still a number of independent retailers dotted around the town. On Wednesdays and Saturdays there is even more to see as the street-market is still a thriving concern.

The Two Rivers project won an award for Staines. The town was also presented with a Town Centre Environmental Award in 2003, an honour prompted by the pedestrianisation of the High Street the previous year. All motor vehicles had been excluded from the street by 2000, and the process was now complete. The old Victorian drinking-fountain, which had been banished to Moor Lane in the 1950s, was reinstated near the Iron Bridge.

The Memorial Gardens were also given a makeover in 2002. They were furnished with

NORRIS ROAD, LEADING TOWARDS TWO RIVERS
2004 S175718k (Russell Thompson)

Staines Artwalk leaflet reproduced with the permission of Spelthorne Borough Council - Copies of the leaflet can be obtained by phoning 01784 446433 or can be downloaded from the council's website at www.spelthorne.gov.uk.

SPELTHORNE COUNCIL'S BROCHURE FOR STAINES PUBLIC ART TRAIL
ZZZ00964

ONE OF THE SWAN ARCHES, DESIGNED BY ANTONY AND SIMON ROBINSON 2004
S175719k (Russell Thompson)

Did you know?

Famous Residents

Staines has had its fair share of famous residents. The playwright Alan Ayckbourn attended school here, as did Christine Keeler, the femme fatale at the centre of the Profumo scandal. Richard 'Stinker' Murdoch, the radio personality who acted as a foil for Arthur Askey on shows like Bandwagon, not only lived in Staines, but also had a road named after him. This is Murdoch Close, off Cherry Orchard.

a new fountain, and the striking 'flying swan' archways on Market Square and Thames Street. The swan theme was continued in the metallic sculpture, Origami Swans, whose shiny surface reflects, in a literal sense, the live birds on the river. These artistic embellishments were part of a plan to fill Staines with sculptures, mosaics and relief-carvings that make reference to the town's past and its natural setting.

The natural setting is still perfectly embodied in Staines Moor. Somehow it maintains its identity on the brink of Heathrow, the M25 and various gravel-workings. Designated a Site of Special Scientific Interest, it has largely been untouched by cultivation for the past

Swan Upping

Laleham, River Thames 1934 86342

Traditionally, all swans belong to the Crown. In the 1470s, however, a certain number of Thames swans were allotted to the Vintners' and Dyers' Guilds of the City of London.

Around the third week in July, an annual ceremony called Swan Upping takes place. The Queen's Swanherd and representatives of the two guilds sail up the river, inspecting the swans and ascertaining their ownership. All birds are identified by a system of nicks cut into their beaks, cygnets inheriting the same owners as their parents. The flotilla once sailed from Blackfriars Bridge to Henley. It now begins at Sunbury, and thus passes through Laleham and Staines. The boats, two for each of the groups, are distinguished by the coloured liveries worn by their occupants, and by the flags flown at their prows. The Swanherd and the two guild-wardens are also responsible for the birds' welfare throughout the year.

thousand years. Extending over 217 acres, it is the largest area of alluvial pasture in Surrey, and is home to 295 species of plant and 130 species of bird, as well as a range of mammals, insects and molluscs. Cattle and horses are still grazed here, just as they always were, though the grazing is carefully managed in a way that will be of maximum benefit to the plants and soil. The Moor also encompasses a stretch of the Colne Valley Way, a long-distance footpath connecting Staines with Cowley.

For most of its route, the Colne Valley Way runs parallel with the M25. Staines is in a position to make the most of the road, being only a stone's throw from Junction 13. With both the M3 and M4 reasonably close at hand, the town still has some claim to be the 'Gateway to the West'. Staines is well-served, too, by public transport. It is extremely handy for Heathrow, without ever seeming to live in its shadow. Waterloo is only 30 minutes away on the train. And as for the river, whilst it is no longer considered a vital artery of communication, it is still alive with scheduled pleasure-cruisers and other forms of leisure-craft.

THE OAST HOUSE 2004 S1752Ik (Russell Thompson)

The Oast House is now one of Spelthorne's adult education centres. This tower was never actually used for drying hops, which, technically speaking, is what an oast house does, but the name has stuck. Harris' Brewery owned 39 licensed premises when Ashby's took it over in 1903.

Back in the town, a new museum is being planned. It will sit beside the library, having outgrown its old home in the Engine House behind the Town Hall. Further south, at Knowle Green, Spelthorne Leisure Centre has recently undergone a first-class refurbishment, and

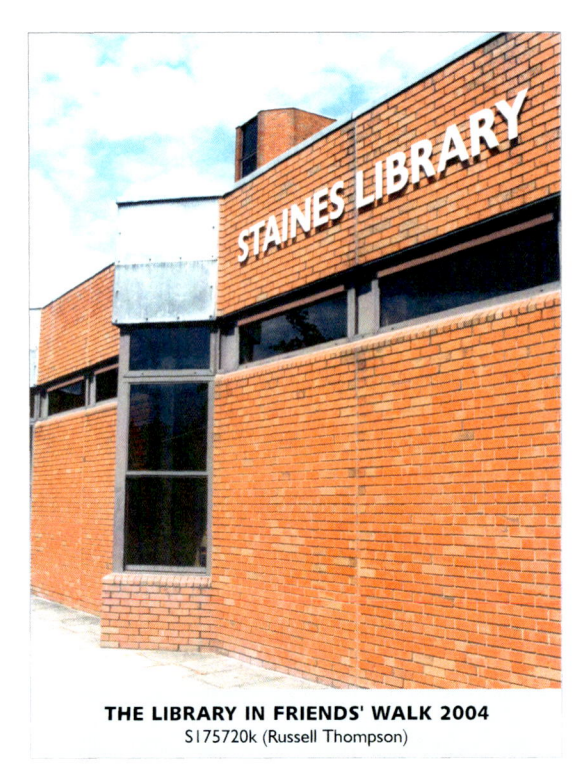

THE LIBRARY IN FRIENDS' WALK 2004
S175720k (Russell Thompson)

now offers an even wider range of facilities. And, for those endeavouring to fill their free hours in other ways, a vibrant Adult Education Centre is now housed in the old premises of Harris' Brewery.

The other brewery, Ashby's, is long gone, as we have already seen. Like the family that founded it, it rose to great heights and then sidled out of the picture. Those great heights are still self-evident in Staines, though. The tall brewery-tower has been converted into flats that look out over the town. What they see is a delta of rivers, a town with an ancient backbone of a High Street, and, immediately below, a new shopping complex buzzing with life. The world, it seems, marches on. But then, people were buying and selling things on the Two Rivers site two thousand years ago, when

Looking Forward 115

> ## Did you know?
> ### Moving the Goalposts
>
> *The town's other 'Swans', Staines Town Football Club, began life as Staines Albany in 1892. Although they played at Hammond's Farm (now submerged by the King George VI Reservoir), their changing-room was a mile away at the White Lion. They had to carry their goalposts to the pitch. In the 1920s they became Staines Lagonda, before adopting their present name. The club's ground, Wheatsheaf Park, is currently undergoing a £6,000,000 makeover.*

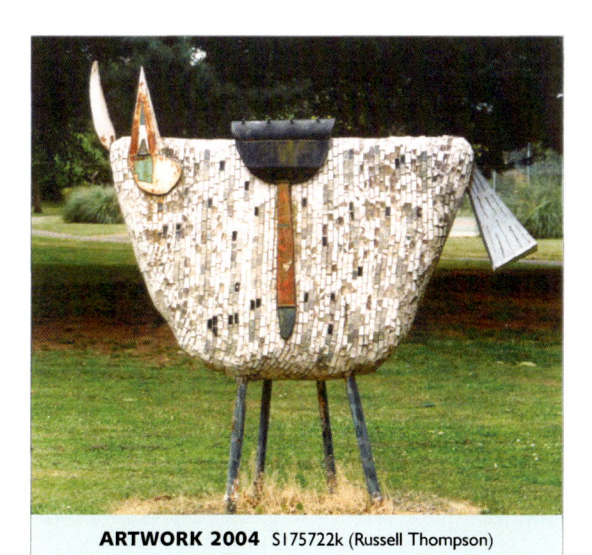

this was just a place 'at the bridges'.

In his excellent 1953 study 'Middlesex', the writer Michael Robbins mused that Staines, 'in spite of its position, remained singularly unaffected by historic events'. In many ways, he was right. But, in other ways, he was wrong, because Staines, for centuries, had been quietly forging a history that was all its own. Just by being there.

And not even Ali G could disrespect that.

ARTWORK 2004 S175722k (Russell Thompson)
Another of the challenging pieces of artwork now dotted around Staines.

DRINKING FOUNTAIN 2004 S175728k (Russell Thompson)

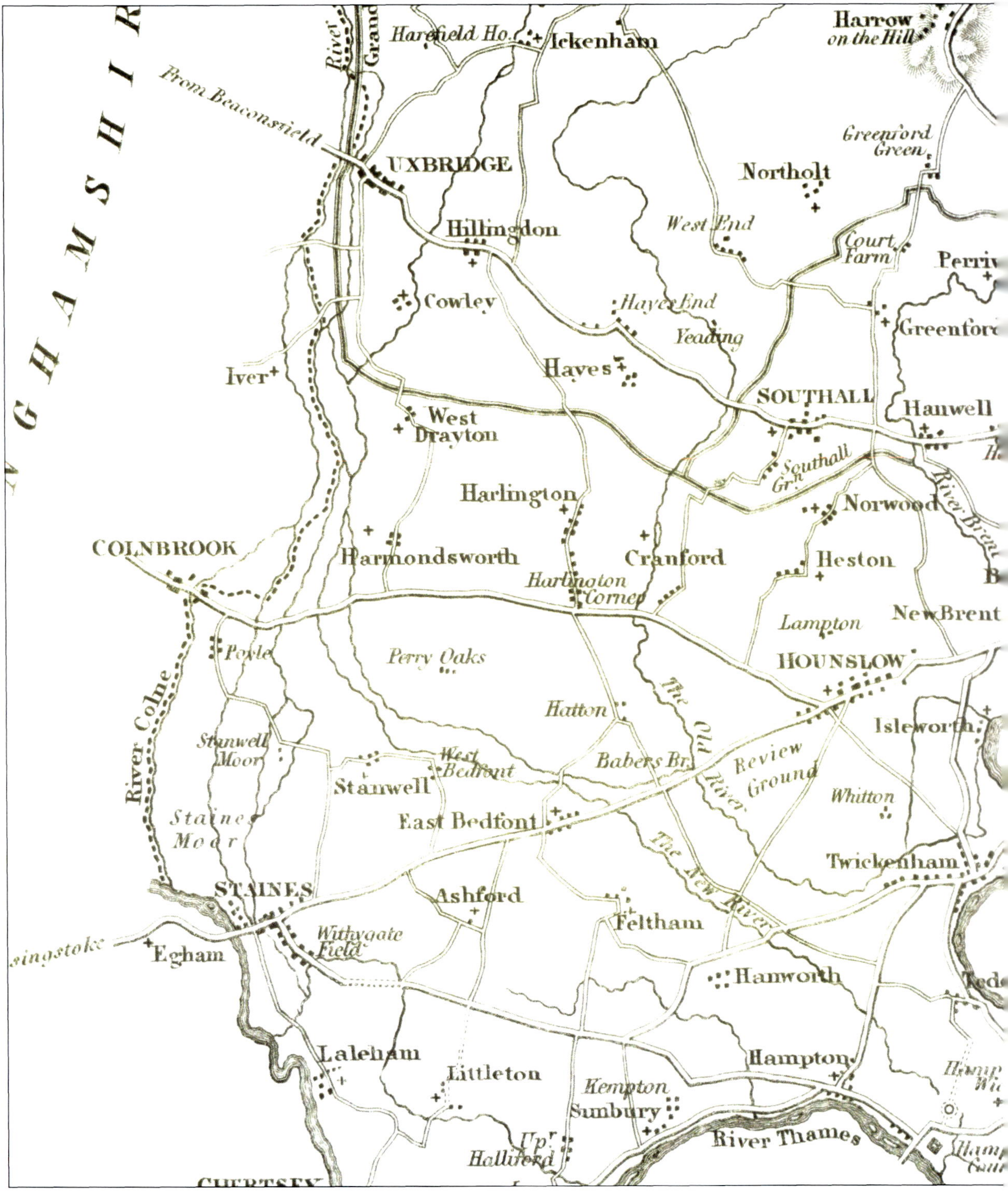
UXBRIDGE
Ickenham
Harefield Ho.
Harrow on the Hill
Greenford Green
Northolt
Hillingdon
West End
Court Farm
Cowley
Haye End
Yeading
Greenford
Iver
Hayes
SOUTHALL
Hanwell
West Drayton
Southall Grn
Harlington
Norwood
COLNBROOK
Harmondsworth
Cranford
Heston
Harlington Corner
New Brent
Lampton
Poyle
Perry Oaks
HOUNSLOW
Hatton
Isleworth
Stanwell Moor
West Bedfont
Babers Br.
Review Ground
Stanwell
Whitton
River Colne
Staines Moor
East Bedfont
The Old River
Twickenham
STAINES
Ashford
The New River
Egham
Withygate Field
Feltham
Hanworth
Laleham
Littleton
Hampton
Kempton
Sunbury
Up. Halliford
River Thames
From Beaconsfield
River
Grand

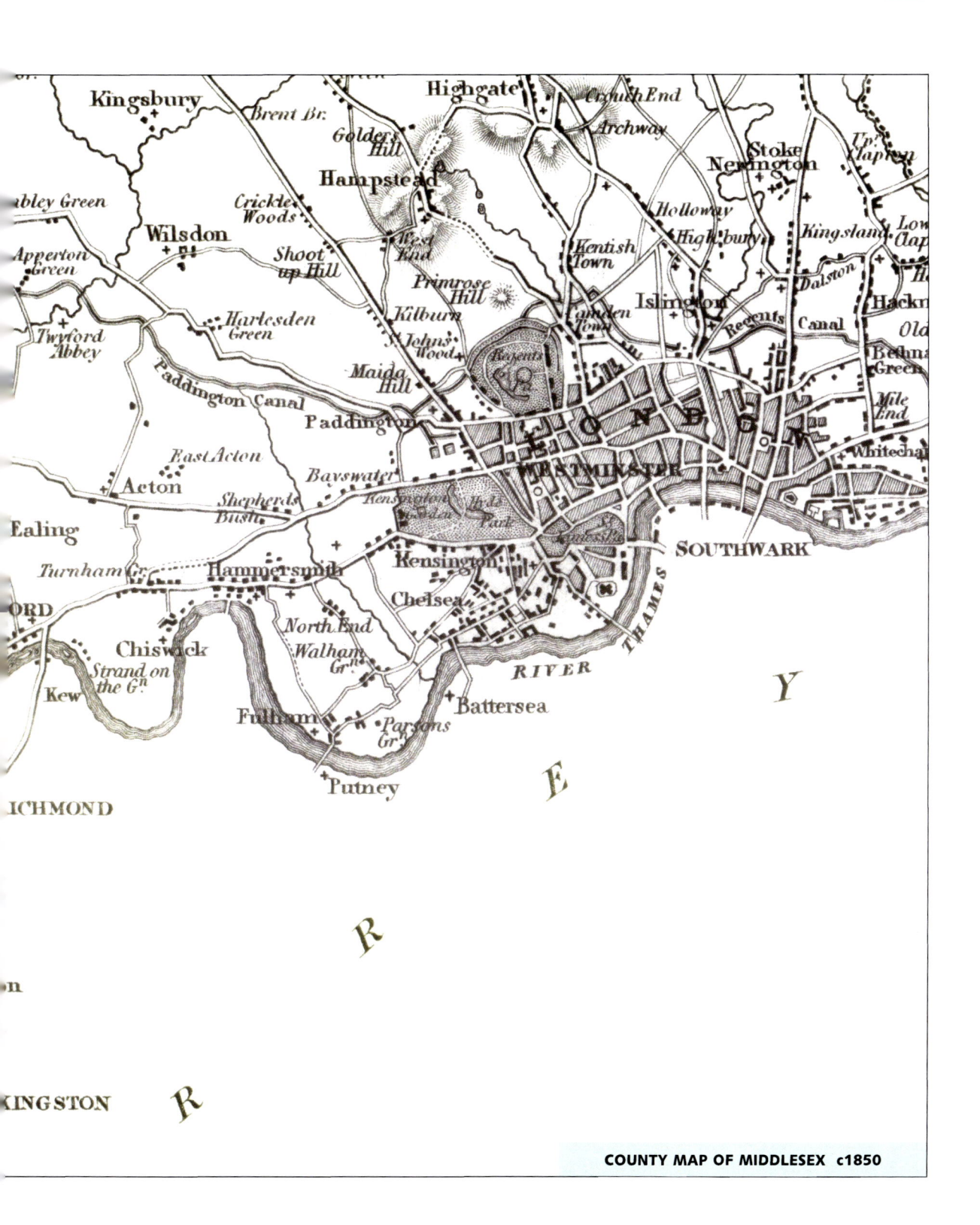

Victorian Staines

COUNTY MAP OF MIDDLESEX c1850

Francis Frith
Pioneer Victorian Photographer

Francis Frith, founder of the world-famous photographic archive, was a multi-talented man. A devout Quaker and a highly successful Victorian businessman, he was philosophical by nature and pioneering in outlook. By 1855 he had already established a wholesale grocery business in Liverpool, and sold it for the astonishing sum of £200,000, which is the equivalent today of over £15,000,000. Now in his thirties, and captivated by the new science of photography, Frith set out on a series of pioneering journeys up the Nile and to the Near East.

He was the first photographer to venture beyond the sixth cataract of the Nile. Africa was still the mysterious 'Dark Continent', and Stanley and Livingstone's historic meeting was a decade into the future. The conditions for picture taking confound belief. He laboured for hours in his wicker dark-room in the sweltering heat of the desert, while the volatile chemicals fizzed dangerously in their trays. Back in London he exhibited his photographs and was 'rapturously cheered' by members of the Royal Society. His reputation as a photographer was made overnight.

By the 1870s the railways had threaded their way across the country, and Bank Holidays and half-day Saturdays had been made obligatory by Act of Parliament. All of a sudden the working man and his family were able to enjoy days out, take holidays, and see a little more of the world.

With typical business acumen, Francis Frith foresaw that these new tourists would enjoy having souvenirs to commemorate their days out. For the next thirty years he travelled the country by train and by pony and trap, producing fine photographs of seaside resorts and beauty spots that were keenly bought by millions of Victorians. These prints were painstakingly pasted into family albums and pored over during the dark nights of winter, rekindling precious memories of summer excursions. Frith's studio was soon supplying retail shops all over the country, and by 1890 F Frith & Co had become the greatest specialist photographic publishing company in the world, with over 2,000 sales outlets, and pioneered the picture postcard.

Francis Frith had died in 1898 at his villa in Cannes, his great project still growing. By 1970 the archive he created contained over a third of a million pictures showing 7,000 British towns and villages.

Frith's legacy to us today is of immense significance and value, for the magnificent archive of evocative photographs he created provides a unique record of change in the cities, towns and villages throughout Britain over a century and more. Frith and his fellow studio photographers revisited locations many times down the years to update their views, compiling for us an enthralling and colourful pageant of British life and character.

We are fortunate that Frith was dedicated to recording the minutiae of everyday life. For it is this sheer wealth of visual data, the painstaking chronicle of changes in dress, transport, street layouts, buildings, housing and landscape that captivates us so much today, offering us a powerful link with the past and with the lives of our ancestors.

Computers have now made it possible for Frith's many thousands of images to be accessed almost instantly. The archive offers every one of us an opportunity to examine the places where we and our families have lived and worked down the years. Its images, depicting our shared past, are now bringing pleasure and enlightenment to millions around the world a century and more after his death. For further information visit: **www.francisfrith.com**

FRITH PRODUCTS & SERVICES

Francis Frith would doubtless be pleased to know that the pioneering publishing venture he started in 1860 still continues today. Over a hundred and forty years later, The Francis Frith Collection continues in the same innovative tradition and is now one of the foremost publishers of vintage photographs in the world. Some of the current activities include:

INTERIOR DECORATION

Today Frith's photographs can be seen framed and as giant wall murals in thousands of pubs, restaurants, hotels, banks, retail stores and other public buildings throughout the country. In every case they enhance the unique local atmosphere of the places they depict and provide reminders of gentler days in an increasingly busy and frenetic world.

PRODUCT PROMOTIONS

Frith products are used by many major companies to promote the sales of their own products or to reinforce their own history and heritage. Frith promotions have been used by Hovis bread, Courage beers, Scots Porage Oats, Colman's mustard, Cadbury's foods, Mellow Birds coffee, Dunhill pipe tobacco, Guinness, and Bulmer's Cider.

GENEALOGY AND FAMILY HISTORY

As the interest in family history and roots grows world-wide, more and more people are turning to Frith's photographs of Great Britain for images of the towns, villages and streets where their ancestors lived; and, of course, photographs of the churches and chapels where their ancestors were christened, married and buried are an essential part of every genealogy tree and family album.

FRITH PRODUCTS

All Frith photographs are available Framed or just as Mounted Prints and Posters (size 23 x 16 inches). These may be ordered from the address below. Other products available are - Address Books, Calendars, Jigsaws, Canvas Prints, Postcards and local and prestige books.

THE INTERNET

Already ninety thousand Frith photographs can be viewed and purchased on the internet through the Frith websites and a myriad of partner sites.

For more detailed information on Frith products, look at this site:
www.francisfrith.com

See the complete list of Frith Books at: www.francisfrith.com
This web site is regularly updated with the latest list of publications from The Francis Frith Collection. If you wish to buy books relating to another part of the country that your local bookshop does not stock, you may purchase on-line.

For further information, trade, or author enquiries please contact us at the address below:
The Francis Frith Collection, Unit 6, Oakley Business Park, Wylye Road, Dinton, Wiltshire SP3 5EU.
Tel: +44 (0)1722 716 376 Fax: +44 (0)1722 716 881 Email: sales@francisfrith.co.uk

---

See Frith products on the internet at www.francisfrith.com

FREE PRINT OF YOUR CHOICE
CHOOSE A PHOTOGRAPH FROM THIS BOOK
+ £3.50 POSTAGE

Mounted Print
Overall size 14 x 11 inches (355 x 280mm)

TO RECEIVE YOUR FREE PRINT

Choose any Frith photograph in this book
Simply complete the Voucher opposite and return it with your remittance for £3.50 (to cover postage and handling) and we will print the photograph of your choice in SEPIA (size 11 x 8 inches) and supply it in a cream mount ready to frame (overall size 14 x 11 inches).

Order additional Mounted Prints at HALF PRICE - £12.00 each (normally £24.00)
If you would like to order more Frith prints from this book, possibly as gifts for friends and family, you can buy them at half price (with no additional postage costs).

Have your Mounted Prints framed
For an extra £20.00 per print you can have your mounted print(s) framed in an elegant polished wood and gilt moulding, overall size 16 x 13 inches (no additional postage required).

IMPORTANT!

❶ Please note: aerial photographs and photographs with a reference number starting with a "Z" are not Frith photographs and cannot be supplied under this offer.

❷ Offer valid for delivery to one UK address only.

❸ These special prices are only available if you use this form to order. You must use the ORIGINAL VOUCHER on this page (no copies permitted). We can only despatch to one UK address.

❹ This offer cannot be combined with any other offer.

As a customer your name & address will be stored by Frith but not sold or rented to third parties. Your data will be used for the purpose of this promotion only.

Send completed Voucher form to:
**The Francis Frith Collection,
6 Oakley Business Park, Wylye Road,
Dinton, Wiltshire SP3 5EU**

Voucher *for FREE and Reduced Price Frith Prints*

Please do not photocopy this voucher. Only the original is valid, so please fill it in, cut it out and return it to us with your order.

Picture ref no	Page no	Qty	Mounted @ £12.00	Framed + £20.00	Total Cost £
		1	Free of charge*	£	£
			£12.00	£	£
			£12.00	£	£
			£12.00	£	£
			£12.00	£	£
			£12.00	£	£

*Please allow 28 days for delivery.
Offer available to one UK address only*

* Post & handling £3.80

Total Order Cost £

Title of this book ....
I enclose a cheque/postal order for £ ....
made payable to 'The Francis Frith Collection'

OR please debit my Mastercard / Visa / Maestro card, details below

Card Number:

Issue No (Maestro only):   Valid from (Maestro):

Card Security Number: Expires:

Signature:

Name Mr/Mrs/Ms ....
Address ....
....
....
.... Postcode ....
Daytime Tel No ....
Email ....

Valid to 31/12/15

Free Print – see overleaf

Can you help us with information about any of the Frith photographs in this book?

We are gradually compiling an historical record for each of the photographs in the Frith archive. It is always fascinating to find out the names of the people shown in the pictures, as well as insights into the shops, buildings and other features depicted.

If you recognize anyone in the photographs in this book, or if you have information not already included in the author's caption, do let us know. We would love to hear from you, and will try to publish it in future books or articles.

An Invitation from The Francis Frith Collection to Share Your Memories

The 'Share Your Memories' feature of our website allows members of the public to add personal memories relating to the places featured in our photographs, or comment on others already added. Seeing a place from your past can rekindle forgotten or long held memories. Why not visit the website, find photographs of places you know well and add YOUR story for others to read and enjoy? We would love to hear from you!

www.francisfrith.com/memories

Our production team

Frith books are produced by a small dedicated team at offices near Salisbury. Most have worked with the Frith Collection for many years. All have in common one quality: they have a passion for the Frith Collection.

Frith Books and Gifts

We have a wide range of books and gifts available on our website utilising our photographic archive, many of which can be individually personalised.

www.francisfrith.com

Contains material sourced from responsibly managed forests.

FF010756